Living Right in a World of Woe

Jack Chalk

Copyright © 2015 by Jack Chalk.

Published 2015 by Antioch Publications, USA.

All rights reserved. This book or any portion thereof may not be reproduced or used in any manner whatsoever without the express written permission of the publisher except for the use of brief quotations in a book review.

ISBNs:
978-0-9967929-0-5 - Print
978-0-9967929-1-2 - Mobi
978-0-9967929-2-9 - ePub

Scripture quotations, unless otherwise indicated, are taken from THE HOLY BIBLE, NEW INTERNATIONAL VERSION®, NIV® Copyright © 1973, 1978, 1984, 2011 by Biblica, Inc.® Used by permission. All rights reserved worldwide.

Contents

Why a World of Woe?. 7

See Right to Live Right. 19

God's will is Right. 27

The World Started Right but Went Wrong. . . . 35

The World That is Wrong. 51

Be Right to Live Right. 71

Doing Right is Living Right. 87

Living Right in a World of Woe. 105

A Hymn of Victory Over Woe. 123

"Would I were dead,

if God's good will ere so,

For what is in this world

but grief and woe?"

~ William Shakespeare ~

King Henry VI, Act 2, Scene 5

CHAPTER 1

Why a World of Woe?

From the beginning of the world God has given instructions in the form of commandments and laws informing His people how they are to live in this world. These commandments and laws are the basis of God's relationship with people. He is God; we are His creation. He commands; we obey. Our obedience to His laws brings blessings. Our disobedience to His laws brings curses and woe. God does not change and God's laws do not change. What God says is right will never be wrong. What God says is wrong will never be right.

We are now living in a time when some civil laws of the land are in opposition to the laws of God. What is evil in God's sight is now called good. Obedience to those laws that oppose God's laws will bring woe to individuals and nations. What is a Christian to do when ungodliness is the law of the land? The answer is simple: we are to obey

God rather than man (Acts 5:29). At this time when legal and societal pressure will be on Christians to conform to the laws of the world, it will be good to take a fresh look at how God requires his people to live right in this world and its coming woe. We must see right, be right and do right in order to live right in a world of woe.

God pronounced woe to the enemies of Israel. God pronounced woe to Israel. The psalmist pronounced woe to himself. The prophets pronounced woe to themselves. Jesus pronounced woe to cities. Jesus pronounced woe to the teachers of the law and Pharisees. Jesus pronounced woe to the rich. In Matthew 18:7 Jesus pronounced woe to the world. What is woe? Where does woe come from? Why does woe come? Why is this world a world of woe?

Woe has several different meanings as used in the Bible. None of them are good. Woe can mean an exclamation that brings a curse of condemnation or judgment. It can mean deep sorrow, grief or affliction. It can mean ruinous trouble and calamity. An exclamation of woe can apply to the one expressing it as in the case of the psalmist and the prophets. It can apply to individual people, cities and nations when pronounced by God.

With the psalmists and the prophets, woe comes from what they observed going on around them. The wicked prosper. God's people suffer. But the greatest woe came to the prophets because they observed God's people sinning and enjoying it. Woe comes to the sinners as a natural outcome of their sin.

Romans 1 gives us a list of things that go wrong when people do not acknowledge God: their thinking becomes futile and their hearts are darkened; thinking they are wise, they become fools; and, God gives them over to the sinful desires of their hearts, to sexual impurity for the degrading of their bodies with one another. Sin brings woe to the sinners. This woe is the one that means a curse or condemnation. This woe comes from God.

Isaiah 5:20–24 gives us a concise explanation of why woe comes and why the world today is a world of woe. The prophet spoke words that apply to all ages when he said:

> Woe to those who call evil good and good evil, who put darkness for light and light for darkness, who put bitter for sweet and sweet for bitter.
>
> 21 Woe to those who are wise in their own eyes and clever in their own sight.
>
> 22 Woe to those who are heroes at drinking wine and champions at mixing drinks,
>
> 23 who acquit the guilty for a bribe, but deny justice to the innocent.
>
> 24 Therefore, as tongues of fire lick up straw and as dry grass sinks down in the flames, so their roots will decay and their flowers blow away like dust; for they have rejected the law of the Lord Almighty and spurned the word of the Holy One of Israel.

After describing the world we live in, the prophet succinctly put the reason woe comes in these words, "they have rejected the law of the Lord Almighty and spurned the word of the Holy One of Israel."

Why is this world a world of woe?

This world is a world of woe because it is wrong. The world is wrong because man is wrong. Man is wrong because he has exalted himself in his own eyes to usurp God's reign and, rejecting God's laws, has therefore become futile in his thinking. Futile means serving no useful purpose; completely ineffective. It also means vain and implies failure to achieve a desired result. Man's world is not a wonderful world. It is a world of woe because it has gone wrong.

Calling evil good and good evil is descriptive of Western society today. This is especially true in the area of sexual sins. Romans Chapter 1 describes society today: "Even their women exchanged natural relations for unnatural ones. In the same way men also abandoned natural relations with women and were inflamed with lust for one another. Men committed indecent acts with other men..." This has now become the law of the land in the U.S., U.K. and Europe. This calling evil good will bring woe on these countries. Politicians, judges, entertainers and media moguls think they are wise in their own eyes. Woe is them.

"Woe to those who are heroes at drinking wine and champions at mixing drinks." Drinking alcohol is at an all-time high and increases every year. Drunkenness is a sin (Gal. 5:21). The heroes and champions are those who drink too much. According to the National Institute on Alcohol Abuse, 25% of Americans age 18 and over binge drink at least monthly. Those are the world's champions. Proverbs 23 asks, "Who has woe?" The answer given is, "Those who linger over wine, who go to sample bowls of mixed wine." Drinking too much has brought woe on the world.

Acquitting the guilty for a bribe certainly applies to the political leaders today who let illegal aliens stay in their country and give them all of the rights of citizenship in exchange for their votes at the next election. We could go on and on about the evil that is called good in the world today. Is it any wonder that this world is a world of woe?

The basic premise of this work on how to live right in this twenty-first century world of woe is that it will be lived under persecution of some form and that the persecution will get more severe as the century progresses. My basis for this premise is two-fold: The Word of God in the Bible; and, what is happening in the world in the second decade of the twenty-first century as this is being written.

Persecution of Christians started with the persecution of Christ, and, as He stated, if they persecuted Him they will persecute His disciples. The Roman Empire persecuted Christians until the Emperor Constantine embraced Christianity in the early 300s. Christianity became the religion of the Roman Empire and then the West and stayed that way until modern times. Today we see more and more of these persecution scriptures being fulfilled. The first century and the twenty-first century Christians show the application of these scriptures.

It was gracious of our Lord to tell His disciples in His first teaching that, not if, but when they were persecuted because of their righteousness and their association with Him, they would be blessed. Persecution from the world is a sure thing for a Christian:

> Blessed are those who are persecuted because of righteousness, for theirs is the kingdom of heaven. (Matt 10:10).

> Then you will be handed over to be persecuted and put to death, and you will be hated by all nations because of me. (Matt 24:9).

When we look at what is happening in the world today, we cannot look in any direction without seeing Christians suffering some kind of persecution. Islamic countries have made Christianity against the law and converting to Christianity or evangelizing for Christ (they call it proselytizing) crimes punishable by death. Hindu nations persecute Christians in an effort to drive them out. Communist countries persecute Christians in an effort to wipe them out. The twentieth century was the bloodiest in church history.

What affects us most is the rising persecution against Christians and the Christian lifestyle in the West. The part of the world that embraced Christianity for centuries now hates it. My purpose here is not to list all the acts of discrimination against Christians in the West that could be found, but to give an idea of how it is showing up. Across America and the European Union it is now called "hate speech" and is against the law to publically proclaim what the Bible says or God's pronouncement on certain sexual acts or groups of people performing those acts. It is considered "hate speech" to say that someone's religion is false. Married heterosexual couples who adhere firmly to Christian biblical principles are considered as unfit to be foster parents while homosexual couples can be. In parts of the European Union it is illegal for a Christian family to home school their children. In England, street preachers are arrested for preaching what the Bible says about homosexuality. In the United Kingdom, Christians operating Bed and Breakfast establishments cannot prevent their homes from being used for homosexual acts. In the U.S., prayer was taken out of schools, Christian holidays have been given secular names, the cross is not allowed in the workplace or in some public places, and Bibles are not allowed in schools and offices. In 2015, the United States Supreme Court mandated same-sex marriage in all 50 states. Ungodliness is, indeed, the law of the land.

In 2010, a noticeable change took place in the language used by the top leaders in the U.S. and the U.K. They stopped referring to freedom of religion and started using the term "freedom of worship." Even the most uneducated person knows there is a big difference between religion and worship. One's religion does include worship, which is private and confined to homes and religious buildings, but it also includes Holy Scriptures and public acts, symbols and inviting others to participate. The West is moving toward protecting only the private worship and then if that worship is of Christ, that protection will be lifted.

It works this way. Things that were socially repugnant and against the law at the middle of the twentieth century are now socially acceptable, promoted in the media, and protected by law. That seems to be the path that Satan is using to remove the Christian witness in the West. An act that the Bible says is sinful becomes socially acceptable as more and more of that kind of act is portrayed on television, in the movies, in magazines, talked about on social media, etc. As more and more people accept the act as something they want to do or see, they demand the right to it, which means that politicians must pass laws to protect it. The acts that follow this path are the ones that conflict with the biblical worldview, biblical morals and Christian practice. To speak against these acts is considered "hate speech" and those speaking against people who commit those acts are called "bigots" and are generally considered to be "the scum of the earth, the refuse of the world" (1 Corinthians 4:13). It will not be popular and it will not be easy to speak out for and portray Christian morals and principles in the twenty-first century. You will be persecuted.

The persecution has begun. There is a move on to purge Christianity from society. This article appeared in the news in August 2015:

> Chaplain David Wells was told he could either sign a state-mandated document promising to never tell inmates that homosexuality is "sinful" or else the Kentucky Department of Juvenile Justice would revoke his credentials.

Ungodliness is the law of the land therefore the law of the Lord Almighty must be purged from the land. Christians will be losing their jobs if they do not compromise their beliefs.

Again, there is a biblical basis for saying all this. Jesus told His disciples in Matthew 24:12 that there would be an increase of wickedness. God told us in 2 Timothy 3:13 that "evil men and impostors will go from bad to worse, deceiving and being deceived." That is being played out before our eyes in this twenty-first century.

The pressure on the church to conform to the ungodliness of the world has never been greater. Some parts of the church are giving in. We were living in the U.K. when the Church of England and the Church of Scotland changed their church laws to allow homosexuals in the clergy and to perform same-sex weddings, thus conforming to the pattern of this world (see Rom. 12:12). They, therefore, lost their voice in society because they no longer speak the Word of God. And they brought condemnation (woe) on those church bodies because of what they approved (Rom. 14:22). The twice-born in the world are a remnant moving toward holiness. The rest of the visible church is moving toward worldliness. The remnant is feeling less and less at home in the world and in the visible church. The remnant knows that friendship with the world is hatred toward God and anyone who chooses to be a friend of this world of woe becomes an enemy of God (James 4:4).

The pressure for the church to conform to the world is coming from the most powerful political leaders in the United States. President Barack Obama urged supporters of same-sex marriage to "help" people to overcome their religious convictions so they are no longer held back from a progressive American view of equality. 2016 presidential candidate, Hillary Clinton, speaking about abortion said, "And deep-seated cultural codes, religious beliefs and structural biases have to change." These are heads and would-be heads of government saying that religious beliefs must change to conform to the ungodliness that is protected by the law of the land

What is a Christian to do when ungodliness has become the law of the land? First, the Christians must have a right view of the world. The Christian is for Christ, the world is anti-Christ. Therefore, the world will be against you if you stand for godliness in an ungodly world. As the above politicians illustrate, those in worldly power will do all they can to promote worldly views. Now that ungodliness has become the law of the land, all they can includes arrest and imprisonment for those who do not conform. In other words, if Christians do not become ungodly in their beliefs they will be against the law. Just as Jesus promised, those who stand for Christ will be persecuted. We can expect that if we have the right view of this world gone wrong. This will be the subject of the next chapter.

My purpose here is not to discourage, dishearten or promote despair, but to forewarn. There will be enormous temptation to hide your Christianity in a closet rather than suffer the ridicule and persecution that come with naming the name of Christ and living right in a world gone wrong. God tells us in Galatians 6:12: "Those who want to make a good impression outwardly are trying to compel you to be circumcised. The only reason they do this is to avoid being persecuted for the cross of Christ." The hot button issue today is not circumcision. It could be militant Islam whose goal is to convert the world to Islam, or it could be homosexuality and those who promote it, whose goal is sexual freedom of all kinds. To speak out against either will bring persecution.

When the persecution comes we are promised that God will be there with us:

> When you pass through the waters, I will be with you; and when you pass through the rivers, they will not sweep over you. When you walk through the fire, you will not be burned; the flames will not set you ablaze. 3 For I am the Lord , your God, the Holy One of Israel, your Savior; (Isa. 43:2-3)

Even if we are required to walk through the valley of the shadow of death, God will be with us. Therefore, be joyful in hope, patient in affliction, faithful in prayer. Christians always have someone to talk to when they are being afflicted. That someone is our Shepherd, our Savior, who leads us in victory over evil, even if the world calls it good.

Chapter 5 will portray the culture we are going to conform to or conflict with. It will be so easy to compromise and escape the persecution reserved for those who name the name of Christ. Hopefully, this book will help you maintain Christian character and uphold Christian principles as you live right in a world of woe, a world of woe because it calls evil good and has rejected the law of the Lord Almighty.

> In fact, everyone who wants to live a godly life in Christ Jesus will be persecuted (2 Tim. 3:12).

> Because of the increase of wickedness, the love of most will grow cold, 13 but he who stands firm to the end will be saved (Matt 24:12–13).

CHAPTER 2

See Right to Live Right

Seeing right means seeing the world right. That does not mean that we need to see the world as being right, but that we need to have the right view of the world. In other words, we need to have the right worldview. A.W. Tozer said, "We are twice-born men and women living in a world run by the once-born." The twice-born and the once-born live in the same world but they see it differently. They see it differently because they are different.

Keep a biblical worldview

A person's worldview is important because worldview determines beliefs and beliefs determine behavior. A biblical worldview is built upon a right belief about the Bible and determines and directs our behavior to right living. The consequences of whether or not one's worldview is built on right beliefs and results in right living are eternal.

Every person has a worldview. A person's worldview is a combination of all the person believes to be true, and determines their every decision, action and even emotion. It is the "lens" a person looks through to interpret what is received through the five senses of see, hear, taste, touch, smell and what is thought or imagined.

A biblical worldview is based on the Bible, the infallible Word of God. God's Word is the only source of truth we have and it is complete in its portrayal of our world: past, present and future. It gives us God's view of the world which is the only true view and the only one that will not change.

The danger for Christians in the twenty-first century is that non-biblical worldview ideas dominate modern culture and bombard us constantly from every direction. The education system, media (television, films, music, books, magazines, etc.) and the people we come in contact with constantly present us with non-biblical ways of seeing the world and consequently with non-biblical choices.

Several years ago I was at a conference taking place on a university campus where one of the topics was evolution verses creationism. A fellow member of my church was there (one in leadership) and as we were talking after the meeting her comment was, "What difference does it make if we came from monkeys?" Of course, the big difference it would make if we came from monkeys is that it would mean that the Bible is not true. And if the Bible is not true, Christianity is not true. This person obviously did not have a biblical worldview.

Unfortunately, the speaker at the conference was a well known Christian author and professor at Oxford University. He is the one who posited during his presentation that evolution could be what God used to get us where we are today. He also did not have a biblical worldview. Any secular college educated Christian would have to be very strong in the faith to graduate still holding a biblical worldview.

It is sad to say, the danger of being confronted and persuaded by non-biblical worldviews is even present in Christian churches. In the U.S. for example, according to research from The Barna Group, only 9% of American adults have what would be called a biblical worldview. You would expect that number to jump significantly among church members. However, the research shows that among those people identifying themselves as "born-again Christians" only 19% have a biblical worldview. If you hold the biblical worldview, four out of every five people sitting in front or behind you in church do not share the same worldview. That means that you cannot carry on a meaningful conversation with them, whether you try to talk about Christian or secular topics. That is with 80% of the people you go to church with! In churches where the pastor preaches and teaches the biblical worldview, the percentage would be much higher, of course. But with 80% of all born-again Christians not holding the biblical worldview the number of churches teaching the biblical worldview are few and far between.

Seeing the world with a biblical worldview

Seeing the world in the right way, the way it really is, is crucial to being able to live right in it. The right way to see the world is to see it the way God sees it. The way God sees it is given to us in the Bible and is called the biblical worldview. As the world, especially society in the

West, has given up its knowledge of God, it has given up its correct view of the world resulting in people of the world living in deception, calling evil good and good evil, and making gods out of things in the world.

You can see this in the large number of people who now believe that nature, the environment, and animals have equal or more rights than human beings. The biblical account of physical creation gives an order with human beings at the top. That is the biblical worldview of earthly things. The world's worldview is that humans are only an advanced form of animals that came out of some primordial slime. The world does not value life the way God does. Therefore, abortion is the law of the land. That is only one example of living in a world gone wrong. A person must depend on the law of the land to save his life because it is no longer saved because it has value.

There are several books on the market that give a detailed delineation of the Christian, or biblical, worldview. I will attempt a brief overview of it here. From this you will be able to see how differently the world, especially Western society, thinks from the way God thinks.

The first point of a biblical worldview deals with the existence and nature of God. The Bible assumes the existence of God and describes Him as a person who can be known in His nature, attributes and character. He is described as being invisible and personal, loving, faithful, wise, and merciful. But He is also just, detesting evil, and will punish evil doers in the end if they do not repent. People of the world, if they believe in God at all, believe that God is like them, approving what they approve. Therefore, any behavior is right. That is one place where the world has gone wrong.

The origin and nature of man (human beings) is another pillar in the biblical worldview. The biblical view of man is that his nature is a direct result of his origin. Man's origin came about by a creative act of God and his nature came about because God created man in His own image. God used His own breath to put life in the first man. Man is different from the rest of creation, living and non-living, because only man has the image of God and the breath, or spirit, of God in him. Like God, man is a tri-unity of spirit, soul and body. And, like God, every person conceived will exist in some form for all eternity future. A space-time historic change in man came about because of sin which marred the image of God in man. This differs from the world's view that man evolved from a lower life-form.

The nature of reality is another pillar of the biblical worldview. Reality is defined as the way things actually are, in contrast with their mere appearance. This means that appearance does not determine reality. Neither does desire or acting as if something is real when it isn't. The biblical worldview accepts a spiritual realm as reality as well as a physical realm. Ultimate reality is God Himself. He is the uncaused Cause of everything that exists. The world has its philosophic and scientific theories of reality that can never be proven. Worldly people think experiences and feelings are the basis of reality even if they are based on deception.

What is truth? This is a crucial question as we live in a world gone wrong. In the Bible, truth is an expression that corresponds or accords with reality, what is actually the case. Aristotle explained it this way: "To say of what is, that it is not, or of what is not, that it is, is false; while to say of what is, that it is, or of what is not, that it is not, is true." Truth is a statement of the facts describing reality. In the Bible, truth is also the Person of Jesus Christ. He embodied truth, spoke truth and walked in truth. Everything about Him is true. He is truth personified. In the world there is no absolute truth. Truth is relative to situations and personal in its relation to perceived reality.

The origin and nature of the universe is closely tied to the origin and nature of man. The biblical view is that the universe came into existence by the creative speech of God. When man sinned, the physical universe suffered consequences that prevent it from reflecting its original perfection. Thus, there are storms, earthquakes, droughts, etc. Science can never prove origins and the best the world can come up with to explain how something can come from nothing is the "Big Bang" that can never be proven. The biblical view is that God spoke the world into existence and is continuously involved in the events taking place in an orderly, but not determined, universe.

Another pillar of the biblical worldview is the existence of miracles. The biblical view is that natural laws are descriptions of the regular way God works in the universe, but they do not prescribe how God must work. Events manifesting God's actions contrary to natural laws are supernatural and are called miracles. Miracles are necessary for Christianity to be believable. The world gone wrong does not believe in miracles and therefore, has no hope. Only the miraculous intervention of God will make this world better.

The existence of evil has been the world's excuse for not accepting the existence of a good and all-powerful God. The world sees no purpose for evil. The biblical view is that moral evil is the cause of the existence of physical or natural evil in the world. The Bible recognizes that God may and does use natural evil for His own ends, but also recognizes that God does not will it for this purpose. The Christian faith would be hopeless if we did not believe that

God can cause all things to work for good (Rom. 8:28). The world does not understand that if evil did not exist nothing would be considered good; all would be normal.

The existence and source of moral values is another area of conflict between the biblical worldview and how the world views itself. The world says morality is self-determined and no standards exist that come from another world. The biblical view is that there are moral values and standards that are objective and not self-determined. Some things are right and wrong whether or not anyone believes them to be right or wrong. Whether they are right or wrong does not change with the times. The source of these objective moral values is God, whose nature is perfectly holy and good. God's moral nature is expressed to us in the form of divine commands, which constitute our moral duties or obligations to act as God would act. These commands are given to humanity in the Bible.

Finally, in this brief summary of some key elements of the biblical worldview, the critical area in which the world has gone wrong, and actually has never been right, is the exclusivity of Jesus Christ. The Bible says that God exists and the only way to Him is through His only begotten Son, Jesus Christ. The existence of God conflicts with atheists and agnostics, and the exclusivity of Christ conflicts with every other religion in the world. To be a Christian and to maintain a biblical worldview in this world gone wrong is not easy and will become more difficult as time goes on. Living right in this world gone wrong requires seeing the world right through a biblical worldview. The next step is knowing the will of God and then doing it.

CHAPTER 3

God's Will is Right

Jesus gave the teachings called the Sermon on the Mount to His disciples early in His ministry. In it He painted a portrait of what a Christian should be like; He warned them of how the world would persecute them for being like He portrayed; and, He taught them (as well as us today) how to live the spirit of the Law rather than the letter of the Law. In other words, He gave His disciples (and us) instructions for being right and doing right in this world that is becoming more and more hostile to Christians.

At the end of His teaching He gave His disciples (and us) the key that will open heaven's doors. In Matthew 7:21 He says:

> Not everyone who says to me "Lord, Lord," will enter the kingdom of heaven, but only he who does the will of my Father who is in heaven.

Only those who do God's will shall enter heaven. Unless it is possible for us to know God's will and also possible for us to do God's will, heaven will be a lonely place for God. If God's will is the key, then it is vitally important that we know what it is and then do it.

Keep in mind that Jesus is not teaching that salvation can be earned by doing God's will. Salvation is a free gift from God and, as a gift, it can only be received. We receive salvation by looking to Jesus Christ, the Son of God, and His substitutionary death on the cross for our sins. That is the first encounter we have with God's will. Jesus says:

> For my Father's will is that everyone who looks to the Son and believes in Him shall have eternal life, and I will raise him up at the last day (John 6:40).

God's will will get us into heaven because we are looking unto Jesus, the author and perfecter of our faith.

Now back to the key. When Jesus said "only he who does the will of my Father who is in heaven", particular attention needs to be paid to the word "does"—the doing of it. That word is the key to the key. Jesus spoke it as a present active participle in the Greek language. It expresses an action as continuing or not yet completed; an action that is done repeatedly and habitually. Does that sound like it means living right in a world of woe? Yes, it does. Jesus is referring to those who practice the will of God. Right living is the key to the kingdom of heaven.

God's will: one or many?

Many Christians wonder if God has a Plan A, and if I miss that, does He have a Plan B or C, D, F, etc. if I keep missing His will for me. Inherent in this kind of wondering is the implication that God has different kinds of will, and theologians have been eager to reveal their thoughts on the different kinds of will that God possesses.

Another question troubling many Christians is Plan A. Does Plan A of God's will for me cover every detail from birth to death, including where I am to go to school, university, who to marry, where to work, when, where and what kind of house or car to buy? When God spoke through the prophet Jeremiah and told the nation of Israel "For I know the plans I have for you," did He mean every minute detail of every citizen of that nation?

Theologians have attributed many kinds of will to God. These include perfect will, permissive will, prescriptive will, directive will, sovereign will, and many more. A close examination will reveal that they are not so much different "wills", but different "ways", different ways that God deals with us. He does permit us to sin; He does prescribe ways of behavior in the Bible; He does give us principles and precepts in the Bible; He has revealed to us what pleases Him; He does direct our daily lives by the Holy Spirit; and, He does accomplish things for us that we do not even know about. These are things that God does by His own will and His own will for Himself is perfect because He is perfect.

If things God wills for Himself to do are perfect because He is perfect, then things that He wills for us to do are also perfect because He is perfect and cannot will anything imperfect. That means that God only has a perfect will. Romans 12:2 tells us that God's will is good, pleasing and perfect. That means that it is good, pleasing and perfect for God, and it is good, pleasing and perfect for us if we follow God's will.

The idea of God having a permissive will is prevalent among Christians today. God having a permissive will that allows people to sin is not a biblical concept. To permit something to happen is not the same thing as willing (or wanting) something to happen. In God's perfect wisdom, His perfect will for Himself is to allow human beings a free will to disobey or violate His perfect will for them. It is not God's permission to sin; it is God's allowing people to sin against His permission. To give permission is to say, "Yes, you can." God never says that in regard to sin. He says, "No, you cannot." But He gives us the freedom to choose. God's will is never permissive for us to disobey His commandments. God's will is for Christians to live right in a world gone wrong.

God's guidance to right living

Life brings the necessity of making one decision after another. If we want to make the right decisions, the ones that glorify God and therefore bring blessings to us and others, we need guidance in our decisions. That guidance needs to come from God because only He knows what will be the consequences of our decisions. Choices have consequences. If we want God's will to be done in everything, then we need Him to guide us in our choices.

To make wise choices we need wisdom. We want God's choices so we need God's wisdom. God's wisdom is given for the asking through prayer according to James 1:5, "If any of you lacks wisdom, he should ask God, who gives generously to all without fault, and it will be given to him."

When in doubt, pray. Pray without ceasing. God will reveal His will to us when we pray. "For the eyes of the Lord are on the righteous and his ears are attentive to their prayers..." (1 Pet. 3:12). God's guidance is God's promise to us in His Word.

> I will instruct thee and teach thee in the way which thou shalt go: I will guide thee with mine eye (Ps. 32:8 KJV).

> Whether you turn to the right or to the left, your ears will hear a voice behind you saying, "This is the way; walk in it" (Isa. 30:21).

The promises of God to guide us are there. Do we trust Him to guide us when the way seems unclear and we don't know what the outcome will be? We will if our goal is to live right in this world of woe.

The first place we are to look for God's guidance is in His Word, the Bible. Knowing and obeying God's Word is a sure way to receive God's guidance. When you are in the dark about a situation, you can look with confidence to God's Word: "Your word is a lamp to my feet and a light for my path" (Ps. 119:105). What more do you need when in the dark than light? God's guiding light is His Word. God's Word gives principles, and commands that, if applied and obeyed, will conform us to the likeness of Christ, which is God's will for us (Rom. 8:29).

There are times when we need God's guidance in a situation that is not addressed specifically or in principle in God's Word. In those situations God will guide us by His Spirit, the Holy Spirit. Jesus told His disciples, "But when he, the Spirit of Truth comes, he will guide you into all truth" (John 16:13). That Spirit of Truth is the Holy Spirit. All true Christians have an anointing or filling of the Holy Spirit which teaches us about all things (1 John 2:27). "All things" includes the will of God when the Word of God is not specific. As sons of God, we have the Spirit of God to lead us.

The scriptures tell us that the Holy Spirit can, and does lead us by revealing God's will to us: "Because those who are led by the Spirit of God are sons of God" (Rom. 8:14). The Holy Spirit leads us positively by saying "this is the way, walk in it", and negatively by preventing us from doing certain things. How can you know that the Holy Spirit is trying to keep you from making a certain decision to go there, or do this?

Follow the peace

The final principle I would offer on this chapter about knowing God's will I call, "follow the peace." That has been the guiding principle of my Christian walk. When I struggle with a decision and the Word of God does not address the issue specifically, I pray and ask God to not let me have peace in my heart about the decision unless the decision I am inclined to make is the decision He wills for me. I ask the Lord to not let me have peace if I am going in the wrong direction and I ask for peace in my heart if I am headed in the right direction for me. If there is no peace, then I have doubt about the decision. My rule is: When in doubt, don't. That rule has served me well in my life and I have never missed God by following the peace because God knows that I don't want peace if I am not in His will.

You may have your own way of determining God's will when the Bible does not specifically address your issue. The most important thing is to know and believe that

God will lead you by His Spirit as you live right in this world of woe.

CHAPTER 4

The World Started Right but Went Wrong

We live in this world gone wrong through our culture. The language we speak, the clothes we wear, the food we eat, are culturally determined. The things we pursue and the things that pursue us are in our culture. We are going to look at the biblical view of culture. Genesis 1–11 tells us the origin of many things, but we will concentrate on Genesis 4 which tells us the origin of culture. In the next chapter we will open our eyes and view the culture that surrounds us early in this twenty-first century.

Origin of Culture in the Bible

The Bible gives us two insights into culture from God's perspective. The first one is the account of the origin of human culture as recorded in Genesis 4. We are not given a detailed account, but a general, historical account of the roots of human culture from which everything we encounter today can be traced back to. The other one is a very detailed account of what was to become the Hebrew culture and is recorded beginning at the giving of the Ten Commandments in Exodus 20 and includes all the rest of the Books of the Law (Lev.–Deut.).

Initial culture

In Genesis 1 we read the story of creation and when it was finished "God saw all that he had made, and it was very good." He put the first humans, Adam and Eve, in a garden of perfection. Everything they needed was there. All they had to do was take care of it. The world started out right but went wrong. We read in Genesis 3 that Adam and Eve sinned which caused all creation to be subject to its bondage to decay (Rom. 8:21). Adam and Eve were banished from the Garden of Eden to work the ground for their food, but the ground would produce thorns and it would take painful toil to produce the food they would need. In Genesis 4 we are told that they had two sons named Cain and Able. Cain murdered his brother, Able, and received a two-part curse from God. For him, the ground would not produce crops that he would need for food or to barter for other things he needed. And he would be a restless wanderer on the earth. The text tells us that Cain went out voluntarily from the Lord's presence.

Obviously, Cain would need somebody's crops that produced food to eat and he would need shelter to live in. People have needs—physical, emotional, spiritual. There are two places people settle in order to get their needs met—a farm or a city. A farm would not work for Cain because of his curse so he needed a city and he built one. It is in that environment that Cain and his descendents built a culture in which they could get their needs met.

What this tells us is that human culture was first developed by an ungodly line of people who were trying to get their needs met apart from God. The text gives the descendents of Cain but no details until we get to the sixth generation in the line of Cain (six being the number of man). Lamech was the sixth generation and he married two women, becoming the first polygamist. One wife was named Adah and she gave birth to sons Jabal and Jubal. The other wife was named Zillah and she gave birth to Tubal-Cain, a son, and Naamah, a daughter.

The sons of Lamech were the ones to really get the first fully-developed culture going for humanity. The names of the sons are indicative of their talents. Jabal's name means leader of cattle, producer, the walker or wanderer. The text tells us that he was the "father of those who live in tents and raise livestock." Jubal's name means "player on an instrument, sound". He was the "father of all who play the harp and flutes." Tubal-Cain's name means brass-smith. He "forged all kinds of tools out of bronze and iron." From these men came the cultural activities of farming and shepherding and manufacturing; the cultural arts; and, the tools to make food and to make war. From their father came the violation of God's standard of one husband and one wife becoming one flesh, and injustice, resulting in a killing of another human being for a minor offence.

The fact that women were mentioned at this generation of initial human cultural development and the meaning of their names is indicative of how human culture looks upon women. Lamech's wives were named Adah and Zillah. Adah means "beauty, ornament, adornment." Zillah means "shadow, shady" [seductive]. The daughter of Lamech and Zillah was named Naamah. She is only mentioned as Tubal-Cain's sister. Naamah means "pleasant, lovely, beautiful, sweetness, graceful." This set the pattern in human culture to value women for their beauty and seduction and to be used as ornaments or adornments for the men. In this twenty-first century the pressure is still on women to be beautiful and to be valued for their beauty.

In studying the roots of culture here in Genesis 4, I have come up with my own definition of culture and we will see this played out in the next chapter. For me, culture is everything man does to get his needs met apart from God. God wanted to meet the needs of humanity and He did that in the setting in which man was created. But because of sin, man not only had to, but wanted to, exert his God-likeness to do and make what it took to meet his own needs.

We are Christians living in the twenty-first century. Has Christianity been a part of culture for the past 2,000 years? I would say that Christianity is not part of culture. Christianity is life, a Christ-like life, lived in a culture and having its influence on that culture. Jesus Christ was born into the Jewish and Roman culture. But He was separate from that culture. Of course, He had to eat food and wear clothes of that culture. But that culture did not produce Christianity. That culture rejected Him. Christianity was incarnated from outside that culture. The Jewish culture was dominated by self-righteousness and the Roman culture by hedonism. The culture itself was humanistic and anti-Christ. Both cultures contributed to the crucifixion of Christ. Culture made it lawful and expedient to kill the One who came to save them. Is not the world system which is controlled by the evil one (1 John 5:19) manifested by the world's cultures?

This puts me at odds with the current missional

churches and much of Evangelical foreign missions. The general opinion is that God developed the different cultures as an expression of His variety and that cultures are spiritually neutral in their cultural forms. If we go back to what happened in Genesis 11:8–9 we will see a different picture. At the Tower of Babel God confused the languages so that people could only communicate with other people who spoke their language. The different languages made people separate into different groups and live with their groups separated from the other language groups. In separating, they developed different cultures (ways of getting their needs met apart from God) based upon the climate and resources for where they settled. God's purpose for using language to separate the people was to keep them from uniting against Him. God did not develop the different cultures, man did.

Man, though he tries, cannot live apart from God. His survival would be impossible. God sends the rain and the sun needed to produce the crops for his food (Matt. 5:45). God also provided the birds and the natural beauty of the earth as proto-types for man to copy for his music and art. Culture is man's way of using what God created for man's own benefit without giving due credit to God.

Hebrew culture

The descendants of Abraham are called Hebrews. Abraham had a grandson named Jacob. God changed Jacob's name to Israel. Thus the descendants of Abraham are called the children of Israel and, also, Hebrews. Because of a famine in their own country, Canaan, Israel and his family went to Egypt where Joseph, one of his sons, was governor, and where there was food. The children of Israel stayed in Egypt for about 400 years and increased from less than 100 people to several million people forming a Hebrew nation within Egypt.

When the time came for God to deliver the Hebrews from Egyptian captivity they knew only the pagan culture of Egypt. Many generations of Hebrews had been born and had died while in Egypt. God's intention was to have a people called by His name who would live in the land promised to their ancestor, Abraham, several hundred years earlier. He did not want His people to live and act like Egyptians, so He had to get the Egyptian culture out of them and give them the way of living that He desired for them and that would glorify Him.

God's way of getting the culture of Egypt out of the Hebrews was the 40 years of wandering in the wilderness imposed on them for their unbelief and disobedience. "The Lord's anger burned against Israel and He made them wander in the desert forty years, until the whole generation of those who had done evil in his sight was gone" (Num. 32:13). What was left after the forty years was basically the Hebrews who had been born in the desert. This generation was cultureless. They were blank slates as far as culture was concerned. To give them a land and to turn them loose to make their own social customs, laws, morality, etc. without any divine direction would not result in a holy people living in a way that glorifies God. These people were sinners. They needed direction as to how to live in their new land and God gave it to them. He stopped them in the desert and gave them a culture.

The laws and instructions given through Moses were to define the Hebrew culture and separate it from all the other cultures of the world. The Hebrews knew nothing about anything. They had been slaves for hundreds of years. They were told everything to do. They did not need to think for themselves. God, in His love and grace, took the time to tell them everything they needed to know to live together in peace and harmony with each other and in peace with Him in this new land He was giving them. So, what does God's culture look like?

This cultural mandate for His people took the form of a covenant (the Sinai Covenant), plus various instructions given through Moses. They are recorded beginning in Exodus 20 with the Ten Commandments through Deuteronomy. The commands and instructions are situation specific and thorough. My purpose here is not to give the specifics but to highlight some of the cultural behaviors and traits God is concerned about. A listing of just some of the areas God is concerned about for His people include:

- Ten Commandments – the foundation of moral and civil laws
- Forms of worship
- Personal injury to others
- Protection of property
- Social relations
    - Sexual relations which are permitted and forbidden
    - Treatment of foreigners
    - Money lending
    - Divorce and remarriage
    - Treatment of women
- Laws of justice and mercy
    - Bribes
    - Favoritism
- Regulations about infectious skin diseases
- Mating of animals
- Weaving of cloth to make clothes

- Styles of haircuts and beards
- Cutting of the body and tattoos
- Mediums and spiritualists
- Respect for the elderly
- Weights and Measures
- Punishment for wrongdoing

In looking through Exodus 20 to the end of Deuteronomy, one cannot help but notice the detail of instructions given. For example, the Hebrews had lived hundreds of years in Egypt. Egypt is a hot dry place. They were going to Canaan (present-day Israel) which has a more moderate climate and has humidity. They would not have encountered mildew in Egypt but they would in Canaan. So God told them how to deal with it in Leviticus 13 and 14. That tells us that God is concerned with every detail of our lives and the culture in which we live our lives.

There are three things that we can learn from this giving of Hebrew culture. First, God is concerned with all the details of our lives and the culture we live in. Second, God tells us what pleases Him. Finally, we learn that God does not want us to be like the other people and nations of the world, those who don't know Him. We are to be set apart (holy) from the culture around us.

> You must not live according to the customs of the nations I am going to drive out before you. Because they did all these things, I abhorred them. 24 But I said to you, "You will possess their land; I will give it to you as an inheritance, a land flowing with milk and honey." I am the LORD your God, who has set you apart from the nations (Lev 20:23–24).

God's instructions to the children of Israel showed His care and concern for them. And it showed how He wanted them to live for Him in their land. Culture is anti-Christ unless it is from God as given in the Bible. If it is God-given then it is a divine command. To adhere to that culture is an act of obedience.

Cultural anthropologists divide the world's cultures in to three levels. First, there are cultural universals that are common to all cultures (food, clothing, language, etc.). Then there is one's specific culture (my food, my clothing, my language, etc.) Finally, there are sub-cultures which are small cultural groups within larger cultural groups (Mexicans in the U.S.).

Another group that needs to be examined is not distinguished by the size of the group but by its relationship to the established culture. It is a counter-culture. A secular counter-culture is a culture, usually of young people, with norms, values and lifestyle in opposition to the established culture. It is a subculture that clashes with the dominant culture. A counter-culture in the youth usually revolves around a type of music and associated type of clothing, and characterized by rebellious attitudes of mind. Members of the counter-culture make people of the established culture uncomfortable. This sounds like what Christianity is, or should be, in the world.

God has given Christians a new covenant which includes the moral laws of the old covenant with Israel. Again, His book, the Bible, tells us how to live right in a world gone wrong. The New Testament contains many instructions about how we are to live in relation to God, each other, and the world around us. We are to separate ourselves from the world (2 Cor. 6:17) in the way we live and the way we think (Col. 3:2). We are not citizens of this world (Phil. 3:20); we are ambassadors of Christ sent into this world (2 Cor. 5:20). These are things we need to keep in mind as we live as a Christian counter-culture in this world gone wrong.

How the World Went Wrong

Obviously, I am writing from a biblical worldview and seeing the contemporary culture from that perspective. I inherited my worldview from my father, and he from his, and it was basically the same worldview I encountered in society when I was old enough to leave home and go to elementary school and then on to high school. I graduated from high school in 1965 and it was in that time period that the culture and the worldview behind that culture in the U.S. and the West started changing radically and quickly.

There is an old hymn of the church titled, "This is my Father's World." This is no longer my father's world, but it is still my Father's world. That is the foundation of the worldview we hold on to in the midst of what is going on around us. The last thirty years have brought in the most radical and most rapid changes in culture in the history of the West. This is being written in the second decade of the twenty-first century and even the last ten years have seen Western culture turned upside down on many issues.

How radical are the changes? What had been scorned by society, considered too bad to mention in the media, and against the law since the founding of the U.S. and for centuries in Europe, is now, within the first decade of the twenty-first century, socially acceptable, promoted in the media and protected by law—homosexuality. This is not a race or gender issue. It is a morality issue. Society has shucked its morals. That which is evil is called good. My point here is that this societal reversal has been lightning-quick as far as cultural change goes, and no doubt there will be more to come. When society crosses the line dividing natural and unnatural, moral and immoral, there are no other lines to cross. If one group has been given rights protected by law to have sex with whoever they want, how could another group be denied the same right to have sex with whomever or whatever they want. This is only one of many twenty-first century manifestations of changes in the Western worldview and culture that started a few centuries ago.

What we inherited from the eighteenth, nineteenth and twentieth centuries

These centuries encompass the Age of Enlightenment, the Age of Reason, and are generally called Modernity. Prior to this time, theology dominated the intellectual aspects of Western culture. Christian theologians all basically held the biblical worldview that all of reality was an ordered whole. The order consisted of God at the top, and then angelic beings, human beings a little lower than the angels (Ps. 8:5), animals, and the physical earth. God created all things except Himself and theologians taught that God continues to be involved in human lives and human events, directing the flow of history to His appointed end. Divine revelation functioned as the final judge of truth and the human task was to seek understanding of the truth God revealed. This theocratic worldview was radically altered during our centuries under review.

The Enlightenment and Age of Reason brought profound changes to Western culture. The changes were subtle and were not really intended by the ones who got them going. As the names Enlightenment and Reason imply, the focus of this era became the human mind and human reason as the final source and judge of truth, rather than external authorities such as the Bible or the church. In philosophy, the source of knowledge changed from divine revelation to experience, the truth of which arises from the individual's unique point of view. The human being is a substance that thinks (Philosopher Descartes: *Cogito ergo sum* – "I think, therefore I am.") as an autonomous rational being.

In science, Copernicus made the bold declaration that the earth is not the centre of the universe. This contradicted the church's view of the cosmos being heaven above earth and hell beneath the earth. He did not mean to contradict the church; he just reported what he observed. Copernicus based his declaration upon certain measurements taken from his observation of the movement of heavenly bodies. This became the basis of the scientific method of observation, theory and testing that was to put human reason on the throne of humanity.

Isaac Newton was another scientist that meant well. Newton was a Christian and he believed "the heavens declare the glory of God," and he wanted to discover how they did that. He believed that the universe was an orderly machine and that the behavior of objects could be determined by the discovery of the fundamental natural laws that governed them. He believed that by discovering the laws built into the universe, it would only enhance man's sense of the greatness of God. His science had a theological end. Unfortunately, in the period that followed, philosophy's rational, thinking man living in Newton's mechanical universe elevated the scientist as the one who declares truth rather than the theologian or the Bible. If God remained in the worldview of a philosopher or scientist, He was a God of the deist, who believed that the existence of God can be known through reason and observation of the natural world, but that God does not intervene in the natural world and is remote from it.

The natural man that believes his own reason can discover truth does not need a God to reveal truth. And like the rich man who does not need God to supply his physical needs, he soon concludes he does not need God at all. This period marked the end of the dominant influence of the church in Western culture. Religion came to be divided into either natural religion or revealed religion. Natural religion was based on the God of nature and the moral laws accessed through human reason. Revealed religion was based upon the Bible and church doctrines that had been believed for centuries. In the end, natural religion won the day, and fulfilled prophecy and miracles were lost. The God of nature gave way to Nature and human reason. The supernatural was branded as superstition. Eventually, God was declared dead.

The Modern era gave humans a new role in society and the individual human new power. The phrase "knowledge is power" became popular. By the eighteenth century the idea that the human mind is a blank slate (*tabula rasa*) at birth gained prominence. Philosopher John Locke wrote that the mind of individuals was born blank without any rules for processing data and that data is added and rules for processing formed solely by ones sensory experience. From this, according to Locke, it follows that individuals have the freedom to author their own souls and define the content of their character but cannot deny they are only humans. The idea of a free self-authored mind combined with an unchangeable human nature lead to Locke's doctrine of "natural rights" which we hear so much about today. The "blank slate" theory entered into the theories of psychoanalysis developed by Sigmund Freud in the nineteenth and twentieth centuries. He believed that psychological problems could be traced back to what was entered on that blank slate during childhood.

The knowledge acquired by the human mind empowered humans to make human life better with the hope that life would get even better and that meant progress. The knowledge gains in the sciences, especially medical science, and technology gave hope of humans being able to master the world. The Industrial Revolutions of the eighteenth and nineteenth centuries brought forth new machines and manufacturing processes, and steam power to fuel new transportation modes that made more of the world accessible to people. Personal income and population growth increased in the West.

Things were looking good and there was a bright hope for an even better future. By the end of the twentieth century, man had even gained control of the human evolutionary process. But even before then, man was exalted to the throne of his own life. In 1875, William Earnest Henley wrote a poem called Invictus which is Latin for "undefeated." In it he caught the spirit of Modernity.

Invictus

Out of the night that covers me,
Black as the Pit from pole to pole,
I thank whatever gods may be
For my unconquerable soul.

In the fell clutch of circumstance
I have not winced nor cried aloud,
Under the bludgeoning of chance
My head is bloody, but unbowed.

> Beyond this place of wrath and tears
> Looms but the horror of the shade,
> And yet the menace of the years
> Finds, and shall find me, unafraid.
>
> It matters not how strait the gate,
> How charged with punishments the scroll,
> I am the master of my fate:
> I am the captain of my soul.

In all of man's gaining of knowledge in the Modern era, he did the most foolish thing man can do—he gave up his knowledge of God. If all the progress of the Modern era had been guided by God's word, Modernity would still be modern. The main thing that scientists, sociologists and psychologists overlooked in the Modern era was the fallen nature of man and how sin affected man's mind. Technology was used to make weapons of war and increased income only showed the selfishness and self-centeredness of man. Man's thinking became futile. Modernity did not work out so well after all. Progress revealed man's perversion.

The death of God

The death of God in human reasoning left some questions unanswered. Questions like: Where did we come from? Why are we here? What happens when we die? which were answered in God's revealed truth, the Bible, needed new answers. The answers came in the form of scientific theories that could not be proven, but had to be believed because they had become the new revealed truth. Charles Darwin came up with the theory that man evolved from lower life forms and those lower life forms evolved from even lower life forms, and those...etc, all the way back to the first single cell life form that sprang to life in some primordial slime. But where did the slime come from? Like everything else, it sprang into being out of nothing, but without God's help. Therefore, man is only a link in a chain of evolutionary chance and time and when his time is past he is nothing again. His life is nothing and means nothing and is headed nowhere. Man looks at the world and sees that there is no hope for him.

If we look at my definition of culture (man trying to get his needs met apart from God) it is no wonder that Modernity is seen as a failure to deliver on its promises. It was man-centered. Man was the master and the master is flawed. Only a culture that is centered on God can meet human needs. God is not flawed and He is not stingy.

God is also a gentleman and He will not force Himself on anyone. Until Jesus comes back man is free to make his own culture in the world. It is a culture in which man will not be content and the deepest human needs will go unmet. It is a culture in a world gone wrong and living right as a Christian in it will not be easy.

CHAPTER 5

The World That is Wrong

Three centuries of human progress turned out not to be human progress after all. Man had more machines and tools and information but man also had more wars, dictators and poverty. The promised utopia did not come and people became disillusioned with science and human reason as they really did not solve all of man's problems. What happened? Disillusionment leads to depression and despair and lack of hope. How Western society has dealt with this condition has been given the name Postmodernism.

    The disillusionment with the culture of Modernity began manifesting itself in radical ways in the 1960s. I received my undergraduate degree in 1969 so I have lived through the cultural shift from Modernity to what came to be called Postmodernity and its present-day manifestations. In the process of this cultural shift, most things have been questioned and rejected. They were questioned and rejected without being analyzed to see if they were good for individuals or society; if they worked or did not work; and no thought was given to what would replace what was rejected. Generally speaking, the twenty-first century culture here in its second decade reflects the void created by rejecting Modernity, and the bits and pieces that have been sucked into that void. These bits and pieces give existence in the form of experiences, but do not meet the definition of a culture. One philosopher said that Modernity's "culture of optimism" has given way to a postmodern "culture of ambiguity." I will try not to be ambiguous in giving a general and simplified description of current Western culture. This cannot be an exhaustive treatment so I will concentrate on the areas of cultural change that now directly conflict with Christianity.

The Role of Deconstruction

Deconstruction is a concept hard to define. It began as simultaneously a theory of literary criticism, put forth by French philosopher Jacques Derrida in the last half of the twentieth century, and a philosophical movement that questions traditional assumptions about certainty, identity, and truth. It was in the area of literary criticism that it captured the attention of academia and thus, gained its initial influence on the minds of students.

In the real world, words signify meaning. But for Derrida the meaning of words is dependent on other words, the meaning of which depends on still other words, so that one can never find the original word that has meaning. One cannot find it because it cannot exist since all words depend on other words for meaning. "What does that mean?" you ask.

That is a good question, but what do you mean by "mean"? Deconstruction says that in reading a text there is no point of enlightenment, such as the intention of the author or a conformance to an external reality that confers significance or meaning on a text. The meaning a reader gives to a text is derived from the meanings the reader gives to the various words of the text, words are relative and meaning is a feature of that relativity. No matter how hard an author tries to say something plainly and simply, someone can always read the text and mistake the meaning. Since the author's intent cannot be derived from the text, what does this do to our reading of God's words recorded in the text of the Bible?

The following example from art will illustrate the theory applied to literature by the deconstructionists:

Do you see a duck or rabbit? One person will look at it and immediately see a duck and they have to be shown the rabbit. Another person will look at it and immediately see the rabbit and they have to be shown the duck. People can see the same thing differently. The point is that, obviously, the artist intended it to look like both. You really can know the artist's intent in a piece of artwork and you really can know the author's intent in literature. This deconstruction aspect of postmodernism does not hold true.

Another facet of deconstruction that affects the meaning of words is Derrida's theory of word hierarchies. In literature there are often pairs of words that are opposites of each other and they are usually understood to be in a hierarchy, one being higher or better than the other. One word is dominant and its opposite is inferior. Some examples would be good and bad, light and darkness, God and Satan, democracy and dictatorship. However, we can only define one word by saying it is not the other. One word cannot exist without the other and therefore the two opposite words are equally important and the hierarchy disappears. For good to exist, bad must exist, so the existence of both is equally important. To give one word superiority over the other is to empower one and oppress the other. Of course, any kind of oppression is bad, but the opposing empowerment is equally as good. So says the deconstructionist.

As illogical as these two facets of deconstruction seem to the logical mind, they have influenced Western thinking and culture more than anything else. For written text to have no meaning but the meaning the reader gives it and for the dividing line between opposites like good and evil to be dissolved, the whole structure of society is dismantled. Written text defines who we are as a society, usually in the form of a constitution and history books, and the distinction and preference between word opposites forms the basis of societies' laws. If the written documents that define who I am are subject to my interpretation, and if the words that describe what is lawful and unlawful are equal in value for me, then I can be who I want to be and do what I want to do. And that is where we are early in the twenty-first century.

The Western culture that has been in place for about

2,000 years is based on a worldview, a Judeo-Christian worldview, founded on a sacred text. The great foundation of our civilization, the one that holds the sacred and the secular together to form a culture – the secular law – has made writing an essential requirement for human transactions. That is because writing has always been a permanent sign of human intentions and desires. After deconstruction, the content of the text is derived by us and our reading of it. The author disappears and his absence is read into the text so that the reader fills the void and assumes the position of author giving the text his own meaning. We see that played out in the way judges are interpreting the Constitution today.

England has provided us with a perfect example of the reader giving his own meaning to the text. A street preacher was arrested recently for preaching publically against a certain sexual sin that is protected by law. When he appeared in court, the preacher was told by the judge that he was a public menace because he did not interpret the Bible correctly. Will it be long before Bibles are outlawed in Western society so that there could be no incorrect interpretations?

Unfortunately, deconstruction did not stay confined to the confines of literature where it was conceived. The driving force of the mindset has taken over all areas of Western culture. Philosopher Roger Scruton speaks of "the culture of repudiation becoming the official culture of the post-modern university" and I would say it is the official culture of Western youth, who will be Western adults in a few short years.

Repudiation is a good word to describe what is going on in our culture today. Repudiation means rejecting or disclaiming as invalid. It is the noun form of the verb to repudiate which means: to reject as having no authority or binding force; to cast off or disown; to reject with disapproval or condemnation. It is derived from the Latin *repudiare* meaning "to put away." And that is what the culture we encounter today has done to traditional norms and values that have defined our culture for the whole history of the U.S. as a country and in Western Europe for many centuries before. The twenty-first century culture is indeed a culture of repudiation. We will look at some areas in our culture where that has played out.

An attitude

I am going to use the term postmodern and postmodernism to refer to the culture of the early twenty-first century. Some philosophers say we are in a Post-postmodern culture, but they can't really define it (it's that meaning of words thing again). Postmodern culture is basically an attitude, not an attitude for anything, but primarily an attitude against ideas and institutions that oppress freedom. It is a celebration of liberation from traditional values and a celebration of youth. A popular shirt I see on males and females here in southern Spain where I am writing this has written on the front: Free, Young, Forever. This reflects an attitude of repudiation of any moral restraints, of growing old, and of dying. Of course, you cannot repudiate the last two; if you don't grow old it is because you died. But you can still have the attitude, and it is an attitude fuelled by rebellion.

The attitude of repudiation growing out of deconstruction is affecting all areas of society. Nothing is sacred. Tradition is trashed. Our father's world has been deconstructed in the culture and in the church.

The Ramifications of Deconstruction and Repudiation

The ramifications of deconstruction and repudiation can be seen in many areas of culture. I will briefly deal with some of what I consider to be the most radical of the cultural shifts and reversals that we Christians are encountering in the twenty-first century.

Deconstruction of meaning

Words don't mean the same thing they used to mean. In some cases they have been emptied of their content and don't mean anything anymore (i.e. "truth"). In other cases words have been given new meanings (i.e. "gay"). Here are a few words significant to Western culture that have either lost meaning or changed meaning:

TRUTH – Truth is defined as "that which corresponds to or adequately expresses reality, or what is, in fact, real." The assumption being there is a reality outside and apart from ourselves which we humans live in. For the Englishman the city bus is real whether he sees it or not. To the Hindu the city bus is not real, it is an illusion, whether he sees it or not. But whether it is the Englishman or the Hindu who steps out in front of the bus, the bus will run over him because the bus is real. To say "Be careful, a bus is coming," is to tell the truth because it corresponds with reality.

Not so to the postmodern mind. Truth is now subjective, subject to one's interpretation. Truth is relative to one's point of view. One's own interpretation and one's own point of view makes truth personal rather than universal. There can be as many versions of the truth as there are people in the group. "That may be true for you, but it is not true for me" is the mantra of the postmodern attitude. Truth has lost its meaning.

BIBLE – The deconstruction of words and texts resulting in the inability to know an author's intent or meaning has taken the meaning out of the Bible. The Bible can no longer be read as God speaking through the human authors to express His mind to human beings. The meaning of what is written can only be understood by the mind of the reader. The mind of the author is absent. Therefore, the Bible cannot be a source of truth nor can it reflect the mind of God, if He exists. The Bible has been redefined as a piece of literature subject to the reader's interpretation.

MORALS – Simply stated, morals are principles of behavior in accordance with standards of right and wrong. Typically, the principles that govern morals come from one's community or family. For the Christian, they come from the Bible. Today, the distinction between right and wrong has disappeared as linguistic deconstruction says one cannot exist without the other, so they are both equally necessary and of equal value. Morals have been redefined to mean it is right for me because I want it, and it is wrong for me not to have it.

FAMILY – The traditional family of husband (man), wife (woman) and children has been redefined to refer to the people staying in the same residence. Here in the second decade of the twenty-first century laws are being passed almost daily as states and nations change their laws defining marriage to include homosexuals of all genders. Adoption laws are being changed to allow homosexuals (single or married) to adopt little children. Currently

48% of the births in the U.S. are to unwed mothers. In the U.S., 50% of all marriages end in divorce. That percentage will go way up as homosexual "marriage" is included in the statistics. In this twenty-first century, for most people family is no longer a place to receive identity, nurture and security. Family is a fluid series of relationships that are self-seeking and are easily abandoned.

EDUCATION – The University is viewed as a place to be empowered to obtain wealth and its capacity to control other people. The educated, especially the highly educated in the fields of philosophy, psychology, literature and theology are seen as those endued with power to influence and control. Knowledge is power; power to oppress. In an example of postmodernism's irrationality, to be educated in Computer Science is seen as a good thing empowering this young generation to control the flow of information driving the twenty-first century culture. The purpose of education is no longer to obtain knowledge but to obtain a skill in order to qualify for a job and to obtain some kind of power.

WORK – A job used to be a thing valued and desired to be kept. Work meant a career in a certain field that you worked in all your working life. My father and my wife's father worked for their employers their whole working life until they retired. Today, only 10% of employees have been working for the same employer for 20 years or more. The average number of times to change jobs is now about 11 times, but those born between 1977 and 1997 change jobs on average every three years with a projection of 15–20 job changes in their working life. According to the U.S. Department of Labor, one-third of the workforce changes jobs every 12 months and by age 42 most will have had 10 jobs.

The cultural attitude toward work reflects a shift in meaning from career (staying in the same occupation) to job. There is also a shift in purpose for work. It no longer is a mutual commitment between employer and employee representing a secure source of income for families on into retirement. The focus is not long-term, but short-term. Work is the necessary evil to provide the money to buy what I want now.

MATURITY – Maturity is no longer valued as representing a source of wisdom that the young need and desire. Maturity means old, and old means old fashioned, oppressed by traditions and old ways of doing things that have been repudiated by this culture.

These are some of the words that have been redefined and devalued in this world gone wrong. These are the things that help define a culture and help hold a culture together as it is passed from one generation to another. The passing of culture from one generation to the next is another very important process that has been deconstructed and repudiated by the current culture. Rites of passage have been destroyed.

Rites of passage

Nothing holds a culture together and assures its longevity like its rites of passage. A rite of passage is a ritual event that marks an individual's transition from one status in the culture to another. Rites of passage serve two purposes. On the individual level the various transitions ritualized as celebrations are meant to help the person to transition from helpless baby through adolescence to becoming a responsible adult member of the community. Birth, baptism, confirmation or Bar Mitzvah, graduations, marriage, birth of children, and death are family and community events in a person's life, all giving significance to the person as he or she grows up and becomes a responsible adult. All of these events, even death, are celebrations of a person's life, giving that life significance all along the way from birth to death. The very first event, birth, is celebrated every year as the person's birthday comes around and family and friends give gifts and say "Happy Birthday" to give significance and value to the day the person was born. This kind of affirmation is so necessary for a culture to provide for individuals. All cultures throughout human history have had these types of rites of passage giving significance to the human person—until the twenty-first century.

The other purpose for rites of passage is seen on the society or cultural level. In order for a cultural community to continue existing, the people must reproduce and the knowledge, beliefs, arts, laws, morals, customs and traditions that define that society or culture must be instilled into each succeeding generation. Culture is inherited and for it to last the inheritance must be passed on. Rites of passage serve that purpose. The baptism, confirmation and Bar Mitzvah mark a transition into the religious realm of the culture and mark the beginning of the religious education assuring the religion and morals of the society continue to the next generation. Education of children assures the knowledge, beliefs, arts, laws and customs are passed on to the next generation. In traditional societies, puberty and dating with its attendant sexual stirrings are preparation for getting married and marriage is preparation for reproducing children so that the society continues to be populated. The new generation is raised up to be just like the previous generation because the rites of passage insured the whole culture was passed on—until the twenty-first century.

In the twenty-first century Western culture, rites of passage are pretty much confined to the part of society that still holds to the Judeo-Christian worldview and that is a very small part of society and is getting smaller all the time. With so many babies that are not aborted being born out of wedlock, and so many marriages ending in divorce; with so many youth dropping out of school, and the ones who get educated get trained to perform a task rather than educated in the building blocks of life; with religion being trashed; and with being old considered to be a burden to society, people have nothing to celebrate and nobody to celebrate it with. Rites of passage have all but passed away.

Youth culture

In his book *Modern Culture*, Roger Scruton states that the popular culture today is predominately a culture of youth. His chapter describing the youth culture is appropriately titled "Yoofanasia." He writes:

> Among youth, as we know it from our modern cities, a new human type is emerging. It has its own language, its own customs, its own territory and its own self-contained economy. It also has its own culture—a culture which is largely indifferent to traditional boundaries, traditional loyalties, and traditional forms of learning. Youth culture is a global force, propagated through media which acknowledge neither locality nor sovereignty....

The World That is Wrong

I am a product of the 1960s in America. When I was in the business world I noticed that when my generation of workers should have been moving into middle and senior management positions, the executives who were approaching retirement age were reluctant to turn businesses over to the 60s generation because they still had the reputation of being rebellious and anti-establishment. Many of the ones who had outgrown that stage were being forced to start their own businesses in order to be a manager.

Because of technology and the dependence of almost everything in twenty-first century culture on technology, the older generation has refused to keep up and have willingly turned over the world to a technology-savvy young generation. The technology changes almost every month and the adult generation cannot keep up and eventually quits trying, turning it over to the youth. The ramifications of this are just being seen here in the second decade of the twenty-first century. The youth are empowered to form their own culture, and sadly, it is not one culture, but everyone is now trying to be a culture of one. To accommodate this attitude telephones now have front cameras so that people can take pictures of themselves (selfies). They do not have to take pictures of anyone else and they do not need anyone else to take their own picture. Everyone is seeking a self-identity but with a group to belong to.

Youth culture seeks its identity in its music. As the traditional culture has been deconstructed so too has the music of popular culture. Pop music of previous generations had tone, melody and chords that flowed one from the other so that it was a tune that could be remembered. The songs had an existence of their own so that anyone could sing them. Artists were popular because they could sing, but the songs they sang were not them. Pop music today is just the opposite.

Popular music has reversed the traditional relationship between the singer and the song. As stated above, traditionally, a song had a life of its own and the singer was used to present the song. Good singers singing good songs became stars. Most Pop music of the twenty-first century consists of songs with no melody and therefore cannot be remembered and sung later. The purpose of the song is to present the performer. The performer makes noises and performs stage antics that cannot be reproduced at home except in the form of his or her music video. The music becomes the performer, the performer becomes a star, and the star becomes an idol. The idol's music video is the way to worship at home by yourself.

Youth music has created a community in which a fan can belong without commitment and without participation. To be a fan of a certain star is to belong to his or her family. You get to be their Friend on Facebook, you get to receive their Tweets, you get to go to their concerts with your family—your fellow fans that you do not know. Youth are trying to fill the void of no identity, no family, and no future. This culture presents youth as the goal and fulfillment of human life rather than a transitional phase to mature adulthood. Everything is "now", which opens the door to image and no substance; means with no end.

Image and no substance

Since now is all there is, how you look now is all that matters. Image is it. What do you want to be? Look like it and you are it. This has led to little girls with makeup looking like they are much older than they are. This has led to older women with mid-drifts and tight jeans trying to look younger than they are. Social media like Facebook,

Instagram and Twitter are used as a platform to present a certain image of one's self. They are like a personal newspaper and you are your own reporter and editor. Politicians are elected because they have a certain image without ever proclaiming any concrete policies or revealing any core personal beliefs.

In this image driven culture, images change as the minutes change—there is no time for substance. That means no time to develop personal character, and as this condition continues, no time for quality workmanship. Everything is a means to present an image and the images are not real. There is no end to this in sight.

Means with no end

In philosophy, the term "means to an end" refers to any action (the means) carried out for the purpose of achieving or obtaining something else (the end). If actions have a goal, other than the action itself, when the goal is reached, the actions end because they are no longer necessary. The means has reached its end.

In this twenty-first century culture where image with no substance prevails and everything is present with no thought of a future, what are the means? And what is the end? The image in the now is a momentary experience that is not leading to the achieving or obtaining something else (the end). The experience, itself, is the means and purpose of the experience. Living from one experience to the next is a life of means with no end. Everything becomes a means because all ends have been deconstructed. You do not work for a career; you do not save for a house or your children's education; study does not lead one to the truth; increased responsibility is not a means to maturity as none of these things exist as a goal in this postmodern culture. Images and experiences are means with no end.

The culture of this age is replete with things that provide experiences with no ends. Technology is the biggest experience provider. The first experience comes with the purchase. To hold up the latest telephone for others to see that you have it is a great experience. To use it to send an email or text with the signature "sent from my xxx" really adds to one's image. The trouble is, the latest telephone is the latest telephone for only a few weeks. Then a new latest comes out and the experience of purchase, show and tell and using it has to be repeated again. There is no end to having the latest telephone. This goes for all pieces of technology (computers, televisions, stereos, GPS, etc), all styles of fashion used to produce images, and pop songs that just stop, they don't end. They are here today and gone tomorrow. A means with no end.

The area of change affecting Western culture that has had the biggest impact is sexual relations. It will also have the longest lasting impact and will be the hardest to reverse if Western culture is to survive many more generations. Sexual experience has become a means with no end and has been made available and encouraged for all age groups and between all genders.

The heterosexual sexual experience is a means to an end. The end is procreation. Of course, every heterosexual experience is not for the purpose of procreation, but that end must be either planned for or against. To fail to do so will likely produce the end result—a baby. The homosexual sexual experience is a means with no end. The experience is all there is and it doesn't last and has to be repeated in ever increasing intensity and ever changing substitutes. Like the image with no substance changes constantly, the sexual experience with no end has to change constantly.

Laws are being liberalized almost daily to widen the scope of sexual experiences because they are means with no end. This has only increased the confusion young people have over who they are. Are they sexually attracted to their own gender? Are they males in a female body or females in a male body? Even as this is being written the Governor of the State of California, USA has signed a law permitting elementary (as young as 5 years old) and secondary school students to choose their own gender identity for purposes of participating in sex-segregated school programs and activities, irrespective of the gender listed on the pupil's records. Can someone as young as five years old know enough about sex and gender to be put in this position? It only tears down the walls protecting children and opens the realm of sexual experiences to every perversion imaginable.

At the time of this writing bestiality/zoophilia is considered a "lifestyle choice" in Denmark, Norway and Germany attracting customers to animal brothels from all over the world. Sexual experiences, like all experiences in this "now" culture, are means with no end.

The Christian Looking at a World Gone Wrong

This brief picture of twenty-first century culture describes some of the aspects of the world we live in today. It is not our father's world and it will change before another generation can understand it. A Christian living in the twenty-first century should see the world through the biblical worldview and through the eyes of God. This is what will be seen or not seen:

- No omniscient, omnipotent, omnipresent God as Creator of Universe
- No absolute truth

- Certain sins against God being protected and promoted
- Absence of rites of passage
- Youth is exalted
- Family as no longer dysfunctional but dissolved
- Everything has become a means with no end
- Life is the ever-present "now" with no thought of a future
- Life is a "now" experience with no commitment or responsibility
- Things are not made to last long
- Image is all important; substance does not matter
- Fraud, fakes, and deception
- All views are tolerated except the Christian view
- Tolerance means acceptance
- All religions contain truth for their adherents only
- To insist that Jesus Christ is the only way to God is being exclusive
- To be exclusive is to be intolerant
- To be intolerant is the greatest cultural sin
- Sin is an offense against the person rather than an offence against God
- No all-encompassing story that gives meaning to the world and our life in it

We have moved from the belief that everyone has an equal right to their own opinions, to the belief that everyone's opinion is equally right. Everyone determines what is right for them. Everyone is their own god. Everyone is a fool (Ps. 14:1). Evil has become good.

Fifteen years ago we talked in terms of "floating anchors." The things that held society together and that anchored one's life to his history and identity were no longer secured to anything. Today the anchor rope has been cut at the boat. There are no anchors wanted. Society is adrift with no destination in mind.

The folly of this twenty-first century culture is that there is no foundation to one's life. There is only an emotional freefall. There is no family, no love, not even a faithful friend to land on before you reach the total despair of suicide. When the music stops there is silence—nothingness, hopelessness, despair, death. With no music the body has no life because the human spirit has already been killed. It died when God died.

In thirty years the youth of today will be middle-aged. They will have no choice but to continue on with the culture they created and with what they have been doing. They have no traditional family, traditional religion, or traditional culture to return to. The modern church has let them down. Instead of converting youth to be like Jesus Christ, the church is converting Christianity to be like the youth.

I have tried to describe the world we live in here in the twenty-first century, the world that Christians are in but not of; the world and things in it that we are not to love. It is impossible to predict what the world will be like at the end of the twenty-first century, if the Lord tarries. Current culture has no trajectory. What has been described will not apply to, or be the culture of, the small minority who still hold to the Judeo-Christian worldview and who live in obedience to the truths of the Bible. Christians must be prepared to live like a remnant in a culture that has repudiated the foundations of our faith. Living right in a world gone wrong will not be easy.

When the foundations are being destroyed, what can the righteous do? (Ps 11:3)

CHAPTER 6

Be Right to Live Right

1 Peter 2:9 in the King James Version says we Christians are a "peculiar people." Collins Compact Dictionary gives three definitions for peculiar: (1) strange or odd; (2) distinct or special; and (3) belonging exclusively to (as a fish peculiar to these waters). All three of these definitions describe the Christian in the world. He is certainly strange or odd, meaning different. He is distinct from non-Christians and special to God. And he belongs exclusively to a chosen generation, a royal priesthood, a holy nation—the Christian belongs exclusively to God. The newer translations of the Bible use this third meaning of peculiar (a people belonging to God) instead of the word "peculiar." Christians belong to God and, therefore, they are peculiar, or different from those who do not belong to God.

What Makes Christians Different?

In the first place, Christians are different because they are a new kind of creation in the world. Human beings are the only part of creation that is tri-parte (body, soul, and spirit), reflecting the Trinitarian image of God. The non-Christian has a spirit that is not sensitive to the love of God demonstrated by the sacrifice of His Son, Jesus Christ, for the sin that plagues humanity. The spirit of the non-Christian is sensitive only to his or her own needs and desires; they are self-centered. They do not have the Spirit of God and are separated from God.

1 Corinthians 2:14 describes the non-Christian pretty well: "The man without the Spirit does not accept the things that come from the Spirit of God, for they are foolishness to him, and he cannot understand them, because they are spiritually discerned."

Christians, on the other hand, are born again as a new type of creation. They have been regenerated (made anew) spiritually so that they can accept the things that come from God. It is like a radio that does not have a receiver inside to receive the radio signals. The station is broadcasting signals but the radio cannot receive them. When that radio is made again with a receiver inside, it looks the same outside, but inside it now has the capacity to receive the radio signals. When a human being is born again, he looks the same on the outside, but on the inside he now has the capacity to communicate with God. However, it is not a matter of just adding a part, as in the radio example; the human being is made a new type of creation with a different type of spirit from the non-Christian. "Therefore, if anyone is in Christ, he is a new creation; the old has gone, the new has come!" (2 Cor. 5:17).

Someone in Christ is someone with Christ in them and is a new type of human being. Christ is God and for God to be able to be in a person that person cannot have the old human nature because it is sinful. God is holy and cannot abide in sin. So the old human nature must be done away with. The new creation has a new nature and the Spirit of God, the Holy Spirit, can now abide in it. "Do you not know that your body is a temple of the Holy Spirit, who is in you, whom you have received from God?" (1 Cor. 6:19).

Christians are different because they are new creations with the Holy Spirit of God in them. Just as the living God is different from a dead idol made of stone, the Christian in the world is different from the non-Christian because the Spirit of the living God is in them. The non-Christian has the spirit of dead idols; he is spiritually dead toward God.

The second way Christians are different is in who controls them. The non-Christian is controlled by the world and "the whole world is under the control of the evil one" (1 John 5:19). What in the world controls the self-centered person? It is the things he desires but does not have. "For everything in the world – the cravings of sinful man, the lust of his eyes and the boasting of what he has and does – comes not from the Father but from the world" (1 John 2:16). And that leads to trouble in personal relationships. "What causes fights and quarrels among you? Don't they come from your desires that battle within you? You want something but don't get it. You kill and covet, but you cannot have what you want..." (James 4:12). Trying to obtain the things of this world that he wants, that is what controls the life of a non-Christian.

Christians are different because they have given up control of their own lives and have surrendered and submitted to Jesus Christ as Lord of their lives. The Christian no longer lives his own life, but Christ lives His life through him (Gal. 2:20). The Christian is controlled and led by the Holy Spirit (Rom. 8:14) and his goal in this life is to please the Lord (2 Cor. 5:9). The Christian does not live to please the old sinful nature but to please the Spirit of the God who saved him. When Jesus was on the earth He lived to please the God who sent Him. His life was a life of complete obedience to God the Father. Jesus was different from anyone else who ever lived in the world. The Christian who claims to be in Christ must live the different kind of life that Jesus lived and walk as Jesus walked (1 John 2:6).

What made Jesus different? What makes the Christian different? The answer is how they are, and what they do, that is different from how the non-Christian is, and what the non-Christian does. At the beginning of His ministry Jesus taught His disciples how they are to be different and to act different from the non-Christians in the world. His teaching is recorded in Matthew 5–7 in what is called the Sermon on the Mount. We will look at how the Christian is different from the world in the kind of person he is. In the next chapter we will look at how the Christian is different from the world in his actions as he lives in this world of woe.

The Be-attitudes

The Sermon on the Mount is a condensed version of the Gospels and Epistles of the New Testament. The Beatitudes describe the kind of person Jesus was when He was on the earth. The remainder of the Sermon on the Mount describes the rules Jesus lived by. The rest of the Gospels simply record how Jesus lived out His teachings in this sermon.

For example, in Matthew 6:43–44 Jesus teaches: "You have heard that it was said, 'Love your neighbor and hate your enemy.' But I tell you: Love your enemies and pray for those who persecute you." And what did Jesus do when He was on the cross? He prayed for His enemies. Luke 23:34 says: "Jesus said, 'Father, forgive them, for they do not know what they are doing.'"

As Christians we are to be like Jesus. So the Sermon on the Mount is describing what Christians should be like and how Christians should act in the world. The Epistles are commentaries on the Sermon on the Mount with specific application to Christians in specific situations.

Jesus takes His canvas, His brushes and His palette of paints, sits down on the side of a mount and starts painting a word picture of what a Christian is supposed to look like in the world. This person who Jesus is painting is not tall or short; he is poor in spirit. He does not have black or brown hair; he is meek. He is not fat or thin; he hungers and thirsts for righteousness. He does not have a big nose or a small nose; he is merciful.

Do you see what Jesus is doing? In the Sermon on the Mount Jesus is describing what each of us, as Christians, should be like. When people see us they should see this type of person. And this type of person is different from the non-Christian in the world.

The characteristics of the Christian are given in the Beatitudes. They describe the kind of people we are to be in the world. That is why this section is titled "The Beatitudes." We are to "be this kind of person" and "to have this kind of attitude" toward others. We shall see that this kind of person is different, and usually the very opposite, from the other people in the world.

There are certain things we need to keep in mind as we look at the characteristics of a Christian as portrayed in the Beatitudes. First, the Christian and the non-Christian belong to two entirely different kingdoms: the Christian to the Kingdom of God which is within them (Luke 17:21); and the non-Christian to the kingdom of this world which is under the control of the evil one, making it the kingdom of Satan. There are two kingdoms and two entirely different people belonging to them. The citizens of these two kingdoms have a natural tendency to be like the king of their kingdom. The Christian is a new creation with a new nature and the Holy Spirit of God within him, thus leading him to be like Jesus, the God-Man. The non-Christian still has the fallen nature of Adam and still has the natural tendency to sin. There is no place apart from the two kingdoms and there is no loyalty but to one king or the other. "No servant can serve two masters" (Luke 16:13).

The kingdom of the world is a kingdom of eating and drinking and worldly pleasures and desires. The kingdom of God is of righteousness, peace and joy in the Holy Spirit. These two opposites do not attract; they repel each other. These two kingdoms are at war with each other. The Bible says that Satan is the ruler of this world of woe (John 12:31) and that Jesus Christ is King of Kings and Lord of Lords (Rev. 19:16). Thus, the war is a spiritual war between the kingdoms of two spiritual leaders. That is basically what living right in a world gone wrong is about and why it will bring persecution from the world. Persecution is a tactic of warfare and causes many to change sides.

The true believers will fight the good fight of faith (1 Tim. 6:12) not using the weapons of the world, but the divine power given us in Christ (2 Cor. 10:4). We win because in the end "The kingdom of the world has become the kingdom of our Lord and his Christ, and he shall reign forever and ever" (Rev. 11:15).

The other thing to keep in mind is that all Christians are meant to portray all of the characteristics described in the Beatitudes. These characteristics are not like spiritual gifts which are given by the Holy Spirit as He sees fit. Every Christian has at least one gift, maybe more, but no Christian will have all the gifts. All the characteristics of the Beatitudes should be present in every Christian. Now, we will look at these characteristics. If a Christian is to live right he must be like this. And the promise is blessed (happy, tranquil, content and satisfied) are the ones who are like this, even in a world of woe.

Poor in spirit

This characteristic comes first because one must have it to enter into the kingdom of God. It is an attitude of our spirit towards ourselves as we stand before God. It is the knowing that we are poor, wretched sinners in need of a savior. Within us there is no good thing (Rom. 7:18) to offer God and before Him we sense our poverty of spirit. This attitude is manifested in us by the conviction and power of the Holy Spirit which produces a contrite spirit in us.

To be poor in spirit is in direct contrast to the worldly spirit and the way the world teaches people to see themselves. In the world, the ego, the self, is all important. The world believes in and promotes self-reliance, self-confidence, self-expression, self-promotion, self-determination, self-assertion, and self-assurance. The world teaches us to love ourselves first. Take selfies. That is why God could say: "The entire law is summed up in a single command: 'Love your neighbor as yourself'" (Gal. 5:14).

To be poor in spirit means a complete absence of pride, a complete absence of self-assurance and self-reliance. It means a consciousness that we are nothing in the presence of God and we totally rely on Him. It means that we do not rely on the status of our birth, our education or our wealth. We must be delivered from all that. Before God they mean nothing and with them we have nothing and are nothing without His mercy and grace. The way to become poor in spirit is to look at God and His purity. You cannot truly look at God without feeling your absolute poverty of spirit.

Mourn

A Christian is one who mourns. That is one thing the world tries to avoid. Forget your troubles! Be happy! Put on a happy face! That is the attitude of the world because the world does not want to mourn, and the world does not want to have to deal with people who mourn. That is why funerals are avoided and the world spends so much money on entertainment. The world does not want to face the reality of its sin and its destination. So the world lives a fantasy life of television, movies, shopping, sports and sex and denies the reality of God and the reality of sin.

As the Christian confronts God and His holiness and the way he is meant to live, he sees himself in his utter helplessness and hopelessness. He discovers the poor quality of his spirit and that makes him mourn. The Christian mourns over the fact that he is as he is and without God he will stay that way.

But it does not stop there. When the Christian sees the state of the world and its bondage to sin, he mourns. He knows that was his condition before he was saved; he knows the joy of freedom of salvation in Christ; and, he feels so sorry for those still lost that he mourns.

The person who sees his sinful state and truly mourns over it is a person who is going to repent. The person who truly repents looks to the Lord Jesus Christ to save him and looks to the Lord Jesus Christ in order to be like Him.

Meek

The Christian in the world should be a person who is meek. The dictionary will tell you that meek means: having or showing a quiet or gentle nature; not wanting to fight or argue with other people; enduring injury with patience and without resentment. That does not mean that a meek person is not strong or lacks courage. To be meek is a choice. It is power under control.

The world thinks in terms of exercising power when you have it, of self-assertion and being aggressive. The more you assert yourself and use your power and ability, the more likely you are to succeed. The world considers meekness as weakness.

According to Jesus' teaching in the Beatitudes, when we see ourselves as being poor in spirit and mourn over our sinful condition, that in turn leads to a spirit of meekness. When I look at myself I mourn. When the world looks at me and scoffs and makes fun of my apparent weakness, I am meek, I turn the other cheek. I know that there, but for the grace of God, go I. The meek Christian is willing to stand for the truth against an unbelieving world and even to die for it if necessary. The martyrs of our faith were strong, yet meek.

Meekness comes from a right attitude towards myself and is expressed in my attitude toward others. It is an inward condition in which we do not feel like or even want to retaliate in anger or demand our rights. We do not even want to speak our minds if it does not edify the other person.

As in all of life, Jesus Christ is our example. "Your attitude should be the same as that of Christ Jesus" (Phil. 2:5). He did not assert the right He had to be equal with God. He humbled Himself and died for us. It was a deliberate choice on His part. That is the point that the Christian needs to come to.

Hunger and thirst for righteousness

If the world would hunger and thirst for righteousness there would be no war. It is the only way to peace. "Righteousness exalts a nation, But sin is a disgrace to any people" (Prov. 14:34). But the world prefers sin over righteousness and the righteous get persecuted. The Christian is one who hungers and thirsts for righteousness.

To hunger and thirst for righteousness means having the desire to be free from sin. We, as Christians, desire to be right with God and sin separates us from God. The world is in bondage to sin and the world likes it and wants it. The Christian longs to be rid of it in his own life and in the world.

Merciful

The Beatitudes, as well as the Gospel, places the primary emphasis upon being rather than doing. We have to be Christian before we can act like a Christian. Our Christianity is to control us. It defines what we are and controls what we do. "I no longer live, but Christ lives in me." As Christ lives in us we are merciful toward others.

To be merciful is to act mercifully. It is to see suffering and be filled with a desire to relieve that suffering. The story of the Good Samaritan in Luke 10 is a good example. But the perfect example of mercy and being merciful is the sending by God of His only Son into the world to die in our place in order to rescue us from the penalty of our sins. He saw our pitiful state and He did what needed to be done to help us in spite of the personal cost to Himself. That is being merciful. Because of the mercy shown me by God, I am moved to be merciful to my fellowman; to share the Gospel with the lost and to help relieve the suffering of the poor.

Pure in heart

Nothing distinguishes the Christian from the non-Christian in the world better than the condition of the heart. Christianity is all about the heart. God has always been concerned about the heart. More than 800 times God speaks about the heart in the Bible. Therefore, it must be important to God. Psalm 24:3–4 asks the question: "Who may stand in God's holy place?" And the answer is: "He who has clean hands and a pure heart." Clean hands refers to what you do. Pure heart refers to what you are. The Christian living in the world must understand that Christianity is more than believing the right things. Ultimately, it is about the condition of the heart.

Here the heart is the centre of one's personality, the seat of the affections, emotions, the intellect and the will. It is the total immaterial part of a person. As vital as the condition of the physical heart is to the life of the body, so is the condition of the spiritual heart to the spiritual life of a person.

A pure heart before God has two conditions. First, it is not defiled; it is without sin. Being pure in heart means being like the Lord Jesus "Who committed no sin, and no deceit was found in his mouth" (1 Pet. 2:22). A pure heart does not desire to sin. And when sin does occur it is quick to repent, ask forgiveness and be pure again.

Secondly, a pure heart is without hypocrisy. It is not a divided heart; clean on the outside but dirty on the inside; saying one thing and doing another. It is a heart that desires to keep the first and greatest commandment: "Love the Lord your God with all your heart and with all your soul and with all your mind" (Matt. 22:37). A pure heart is single in focus, wanting only to love God and serve God and obey God. There is no difference between the public and the private life. There is no hypocrisy in the pure heart.

Peacemaker

As a Christian lives in this world he must strive to be a peacemaker. Remember, Jesus is describing a Christian, one who has peace *with* God. God has made sure that in this world no one will have peace until they have peace with Him. Peace with God comes through faith in His Son, Jesus Christ, the Prince of Peace (Rom. 5:1). That faith brings the peace of God as the life of God through the Holy Spirit comes to live in the Christian. So the Christian has peace *with* God and the peace *of* God. What does it mean to be a peacemaker?

Christians are ambassadors for Christ in this world and one of the main duties of an ambassador is to negotiate peace treaties between nations in conflict. We are in the world to offer the Prince of Peace to a world hostile toward God and Christ. We are only living right in this world gone wrong when we are offering the Gospel of peace to those that are not at peace with God through Jesus Christ.

To be used as a peacemaker the Christian must be quick to listen, slow to speak, and slow to get angry (James 1:19). Like Jesus (Matt. 26:63) he doesn't speak to defend himself. He also does not speak unkind things about others. That causes strife, not peace. Besides being slow to speak, the peacemaker is quick to remember what he is. He is a Christian, the only picture of Jesus Christ the world will see. He remembers that a lot more is involved in this personal situation than just himself. To the world he represents God, Jesus Christ, the Holy Spirit, and the Church. He represents Christ and does not want to bring a reproach to the name of Christ. So the Christian must not be quarrelsome and he must go out of his way to look for ways to make peace. If someone says something bad and untrue about you, control your tongue. He is controlled by Satan as you once were. Have pity on him and pray for him. Then find a way to help him. By not being concerned with self and demanding our rights, and by being meek and approachable, we invite peace in any situation.

Once it is established in our minds that we are peacemakers, we remember that the only real peace and the only lasting peace and the only basis for all peace in the world is peace with God. If there is going to be peace between people, people need to have peace with God. That is where the true work of the peacemaker comes in. We are only living right in a world gone wrong when we are living and speaking in such a way that brings people to God. That means living and speaking the Gospel of peace.

Persecuted

This is the last Beatitude and the last one a Christian would hope for in order to be like Jesus. But it is the most positive indicator that you are a Christian who is living right in this world of woe. Persecution comes as a result of being the type of person described in the preceding Beatitudes. To be persecuted and to handle it the way Jesus did becomes a positive character trait. He is our example and He promised that we would be persecuted just as He was (John 15:20).

We need to keep in mind that the only persecution we receive for being a Christian in the world is because of righteousness (living right). If we are not righteous in an unrighteous world we will not be persecuted for being a Christian. If the persecution comes because we are quarrelsome, or on some political side against another, or even for being a do-gooder or self-righteous, that is not the persecution of a Christian.

Jesus was not persecuted because He was a good person or because He did good works. Jesus was persecuted because He was righteous and He revealed the unrighteousness of the religious leaders. As Christians in the world we are to be righteous and to stand for righteousness and to endure persecution for righteousness sake just like our Lord.

To do right you must be right. To be right is to have these attitudes and attributes of a Christian given by our Lord in the Beatitudes. When a Christian is like this, right living is bound to follow. The Christian in the world is to be and live like our Lord.

In this world gone wrong, we find nothing even similar to the virtues of which Jesus spoke in these Beatitudes. Virtue is another word that has been deconstructed and/or redefined. Instead of poor in spirit, we find the consuming pride of self. Instead of mourners, we find pleasure seekers. Instead of meekness, we find arrogance. Instead of hunger and thirst for righteousness, we hear men saying, "I am right!" Instead of mercy, we find persecution and cruelty. Instead of purity of heart, we see people doing evil continually. Instead of peacemakers, we find quarrelsome, vengeful people that are quick to defend themselves with any and all weapons at hand. Christians are not to be that way. Thank you, Jesus, for freeing us from ourselves.

CHAPTER 7

Doing Right is Living Right

In the last chapter we looked at the kind of person the Christian is in the world as described in the Beatitudes and what makes him different. In this chapter we will look at the difference being different makes in how the Christian lives in the world; a world that hates those who are different. As in the last chapter, we will look to Jesus' teachings in the Sermon on the Mount to see what He expects of His disciples living in the world.

The purpose of Jesus' sermon is to teach how someone who is in the kingdom of heaven should live. In the Sermon on the Mount, Jesus is teaching His disciples (then and now) that obedience to God's law is an attitude of the heart and not limited to the outward appearance of obedience. As we proceed on we will be looking at various aspects of God's law applicable to Christians living in God's kingdom while living in the world. That law is written on our hearts and the desire to be right with God supersedes the worldly desire to be selfishly satisfied and admired.

In Matthew 5:21 to 7:27 Jesus applies God's law to His disciples. It is important to note that it is God's moral law that He refers to. God's moral law is different from His ceremonial and judicial law. The moral law is permanent and perpetual. It defines the relation that must exist between God and man, and man and man, and therefore defines life in the Kingdom of God in this world. The fact that a Christian even wants to obey God's moral law will set him apart from the people of the kingdom of this world.

The Christian is subject to the requirements part of the law but not the penalty part of the law. The Christian has been delivered from the curse of the law but he has not been delivered from the law as a rule of life. That is why Jesus taught it to His disciples. The law reveals our sin so that we can repent. The law serves as a light to guide our way in this dark world. The law functions like a leash on a dog. It keeps it from going where the master does not want it to go, and is used to guide it where the master does want it to go.

Jesus Christ fulfilled the law. In God's grace He takes our faith in Christ and declares us as fulfilling the law also. Because we are free from the curse of the law we are free to obey the law as best we can, knowing that when we fail, with repentance comes, not condemnation, but forgiveness. The unsaved people we live with in this world are still under the curse of the law and are not free to obey it and they hate those of us who do. That basic hostility permeates the world and we must keep that in mind as we live the Christian life in a world gone wrong.

On many occasions, and especially in the Sermon on the Mount, Jesus expressed His anger, grief and condemnation toward hypocrites. The root word for hypocrite in the Greek comes from the same word used to describe actors of a part in a play. The biblical usage refers to someone who pretends to be what they are not; a counterfeit; or one who acts pretentiously. Jesus' problem with the Pharisees was their self-righteousness and hypocrisy. The world's problem with Christians is the same—the world's self-righteousness and hypocrisy. The world looks for hypocrisy in a Christian because it is that way itself. The press jumps on it when it is exposed and delights in mocking Christianity because of it. We Christians need to keep in mind that the world is watching us and more importantly, our Heavenly Father "sees what is done in secret" (Matt 6:4, 6, 18).

If we are hypocrites in the world, the world will know it and God will know it. The world will mock a Christian who is a hypocrite because they see that he is no better than they are. God condemns a hypocrite (Matt 24:51) because he is a liar and is not really the Christian he pretends to be.

This has been a problem with God's people since Old Testament times. Jesus warned the hypocrites of His day about what the prophet Isaiah said (Mark 7:6–7a), "These people honor me with their lips, but their hearts are far from me. They worship me in vain." The condition of our hearts guides our actions and determines if we are hypocrites or not. Self-righteousness deceives our hearts into thinking we are something when we are not because, "There is no one righteous, not even one" (Rom. 3:10). The concept of self-righteousness is a lie in itself because we have none, and the righteousness we have is imputed to us by God (Rom. 4:24; Phil. 3:9). Self-righteousness is hypocrisy. Hypocrisy is living a lie and brings the condemnation of the world and of God. As Christians living in this world we must constantly be on guard against hypocrisy in our lives.

Guidelines from the Sermon on the Mount

Our Lord was very direct in teaching His disciples how to live a truly righteous life without hypocrisy in the midst of self-righteous, hypocritical and ungodly people. We will look at some of His teachings from the Sermon that should guide our hearts and our outward relations with others as we live in this world that is controlled by the evil one (1 John 5:19).

As we look at each of these issues, we will be looking at the outward expression of an inner attribute. This is the Lord's concern in this teaching to His disciples—His representatives in the world.

Anger (Matt. 5: 21–22)

No human emotion can cause a person to lose control faster than anger. It is no wonder that this is the first thing Jesus dealt with when He turned His teaching from how a Christian ought to be to how a Christian ought to act. And His teaching reveals how awful anger is in God's eyes. Anger is seen as murder and receives the same judgment and condemnation as murder (1 John 3:15, Rev. 21:8).

Of course, what people do sometimes makes us angry. Then we have a choice. God's command for us is "In your anger do not sin; when you are on your beds, search your hearts and be silent" (Ps. 4:4; Eph. 4:26). Do you control your anger or does your anger control you? Christian, the world is watching how you act when you are angry.

Disagreements (Matt. 5:23–26)

The way the Christian is to handle disagreements follows on from the Lord's teaching on anger. Disagreements can very easily lead to anger. It is best to settle the disagreement before anger enters in because anger can cause a person to think only selfishly. The selfish person is never going to agree with anyone that does not agree with them.

Settling disagreements points back to the Lord's teaching in the Beatitudes about the peacemaker as presented in Chapter 6. When disagreements arise, the Christian must be quick to listen, slow to speak, and slow to get angry (James 1:19). Remembering that he is the only Christ the world will see, he must not be quarrelsome and he must take positive action to settle disagreements.

The Christian must have a negative attitude against anger and a positive attitude about settling disagreements. He must be pro-active to start the settlement process and to do it quickly. The Lord gives two illustrations in the passage above; one pertains to disagreements with a Christian brother, the other pertains to a disagreement with an unbeliever. Settling the disagreement is the important thing, no matter the personal cost to the Christian. We must be right and do right. "If you suffer, it should not be as a murderer or thief or any other kind of criminal, or even as a meddler. However, if you suffer as a Christian, do not be ashamed, but praise God that you bear that name" (1 Pet. 4:15–16). The Christian should handle disagreements differently from the way the world does.

Lust (Matt. 5:27–30)

The world and the world's system under the control of the evil one uses lust to drive its political systems, economic systems and its psychological influence over the people of the world. Political systems are run by people that lust for power rather than desire to serve the people. The economic systems are driven by people's "lust of the eyes, lust of the flesh and the pride of life" (1 John 2:16 KJV) which causes people to desire the things they see in advertising and in entertainment media to the point of going into debt to purchase them because they have to have them. They have to have them because, psychologically, their self-worth (pride of life) comes from the things they possess. Jesus taught that one's life does not consist of the abundance of his possessions (Luke 12:15) and God instructs us to put lust to death (Col. 3:5). The Christian is in the world but not of the world (John 17:16) and should deal with lust differently than the people of the world.

Anything ungodly can be an object of lust if the purpose of the desire is not to glorify God. In most of the New Testament usage of the term "lust" refers to lusting for sexual immorality. Jesus puts the context of this teaching in the committing of adultery (the seventh commandment) which was the most common sexual sin, but He gave it wider implications to include all forms of sexual immorality and to include the desire to commit the act as equal to the physical act itself.

The looking lustfully begins with the eyes. Images seen with the eyes trigger lustful thoughts which, if not rebuked, lead to deeds of sin done with the body. Christians that have been born-again and have the power of the Holy Spirit within them, have the liberty to say "no" when lust is present. It is better to forgo some experiences this world offers in order to enter the next life whole and without loss.

The world in this twenty-first century preaches and pushes just the opposite. Life is to be experienced; everything desired is to be experienced. Everything seen is to be desired. Visual images are the means of communication today; much more so than words. Television, movies, newspapers, magazines, advertisements use images as content and their images are designed to trigger thoughts, thoughts of desire that lead to lust, that lead to deeds. The worldly person is manipulated through his eyes and that is the danger point for Christians. Jesus said, "Your eye is the lamp of your body. When your eyes are good, your whole body also is full of light. But when they are bad, your body also is full of darkness" (Luke 11:34).

The Christian in this world does not fall prey to lust and is not driven by it as the unbelievers of the world are. To not do what they do or go where they go will make the world angry. "They think it strange that you do not plunge with them into the same flood of dissipation, and they heap abuse on you" (1 Pet. 4:4). The Christian in the world is different from the people of the world.

Divorce (Matt. 5:31–32)

There is no area of conflict between the laws of God and the laws and practices of the cultures of the world greater than in the area of sexual morality and marriage. In the world the only legal restrictions on sexual activity has to do with age of consent and that is being lowered or done away with before our very eyes. The civil laws governing divorce are called "no fault" and grant divorce to any spouse who wants it. The major part of divorce law has to do with property settlement between the parties to the divorce. But God has a separate set of laws regarding divorce for the Christian.

For the Christian, God says, "Marriage should be honored by all, and the marriage bed kept pure, for God will judge the adulterer and all the sexually immoral" (Heb. 13:4). A Christian who thinks he or she can divorce their spouse at will and continue in a right relationship with God is deceived.

In Ephesians Chapter 5, God gives His very good reason why marriage is a covenant and why the marriage covenant should be honored by husband and wife. The marriage covenant and relationship is a picture of the New Covenant we have with God in Christ and a picture of the relationship between Christ and His church. That means that when the world looks at a Christian marriage they are seeing Jesus Christ at work loving and caring for His own in a covenant relationship that He will not break. Woe to the Christian that breaks it.

The world follows the example of its entertainment stars and politicians; they divorce and remarry at will. They change partners as often as the wind changes. There is no commitment and only a selfish "what's in it for me" attitude. The Christian marriage should be different and the Christian's attitude toward divorce should be counter-cultural reflecting God's laws and not man's.

Keeping your word (Matt. 5:33–37)

Christians should be the most honest people in the world. Christians should do what they say they will do. Christians should pay their debts. Christians should always tell the truth. Christians have Christ in them (Col. 1:27); Christians represent Christ (2 Cor. 5:20); and Jesus Christ is the Truth (John 14:6). Since Christians are the only Jesus

Christ the world will see, when the world sees us they should see a truthful person, a person who keeps their word.

In this twenty-first century, the world does not trust an honest person, one who speaks the truth all the time and is faithful to their own word. Why? Because the world's system is built on lies and the biggest lie is that there is no absolute truth. We should be the embodiment of truth in this fallen world.

Defending yourself (Matt. 5:38–42)

Here, Jesus is teaching a counter-cultural way the Christian should act, in this case react, when offended. He is saying that while the law of just retribution pertains to the law courts, the law of love should rule in our relationships with people. The Christian's duty to people that treat us wrongly is to treat them with love rather than revenge. And what does love require of us? "It is not self-seeking, it is not easily angered, it keeps no record of wrongs" (1 Cor. 13:5).

The law of love requires you to absorb monetary loss and even physical embarrassment and abuse without retaliation. They are opportunities for the Christian to deny himself (Matt. 16:24) and model Christ to this lost world. The example of Christ shows us that only love can turn an enemy into a friend.

Dealing with enemies (Matt. 5:43–47)

The law of love demands that the Christian love his neighbor and love his enemies. Jesus' parable of the Good Samaritan shows us that anyone in need is our neighbor and we should help them if we can. Our enemy is our neighbor because he is our fellow human being in need of what we have—a new life in Christ. We can help them by telling them of the Gospel of Jesus Christ. Our duty to our neighbor and our enemy is to love them. It is a heart attitude and defines Christian character and righteousness.

Loving where love is not returned involves a cost, but it also brings a reward to the Christian. The reward we receive is the proof that we are "sons of your Father in heaven." To love our enemies as well as our neighbors is to act like God. He sends the sun and rain to the evil and the good. In other words, God treats His enemies and His friends the same way. He gives them what love requires. Christians living right in the world should do the same.

Pride (Matt. 6:1)

The Lord is talking about our "acts of righteousness" and the operative words here are "before men, to be seen by them." That is what fuels pride. "What will other people think?" "Will this make a good impression on other people when they see me?" That is why people spend huge amounts of money on brand name clothes, certain models of cars, and big houses even though they have small families. They are proud and they want to be seen by men as someone to be admired.

It is also the reason non-Christians do charitable acts, which Jesus includes in His reference to acts of righteousness. The non-Christian gives and expects some kind of recognition: a plaque, a statue, or a building named after them, or at least a public "thank you." Jesus said that the Christian's acts of charity should be done in secret so as not to draw attention to themselves. Giving is an act of love and love requires nothing in return.

Our Lord is also concerned that Christians exceed the righteousness of the Pharisees and not be hypocrites. We do not do things to receive the applause of men. We do them for the glory of our heavenly Father who sees what we do in secret. The world is just the opposite. The world wants praise and the world gives praise to those who are worldly, those who glorify themselves. The world does not know how to react when a Christian does something good and does not want to receive praise for it, but passes the praise on to God. You see it plainly when an athlete wins and gives the glory to God. The press quickly passes over that in their reporting and changes the subject back to worldly things. Unlike the worldly person, the Christian realizes that he has nothing and can do nothing apart from God. And unlike the worldly person, the Christian gives God the glory for all that man could take pride in.

Greed (Matt. 6:19–21)

The non-Christian in the world is self-centered and that brings pride and greed. The Lord's instruction above for His followers runs counter to the world's thinking. The world's attitude is "He who dies with the most toys, wins!" Christians know that our value is not in what we have but in who we are—children of God, and we are heirs of God and co-heirs with Christ (Rom. 8:17).

One of the richest men in American history was asked how much money was enough. His answer was, "Just a little bit more!" That man died broke just like we all do. When we die the treasures we accumulate on earth are left behind and we meet whatever treasures we have laid up in heaven. For most, all they will meet is the accountability for the missed opportunities they had on earth to use their treasures for the glory of God.

The unbeliever lives only for this world and the pleasure of accumulating this world's treasure. That pleasure is really a curse. It is a short-lived pleasure. "But woe to you who are rich, for you have already received your comfort" (Luke 6:24).

Again Jesus admonishes His followers: "Then he said to them, 'Watch out! Be on your guard against all kinds of greed; a man's life does not consist in the abundance of his possessions'" (Luke 12:15). The world knows of no other treasure than the abundance of its possessions.

There should be a marked difference between what a Christian treasures and values and what people of the world treasure and value. That is because there is a marked difference in the heart of the Christian and the non-Christian. And where your treasure is there your heart will be also. The heart determines the treasure and then loves it.

Christians should be the most generous people on earth because we represent the most generous Being—God, the Father Almighty (Ps. 145:16). He has instructed us "to be rich in good deeds, and to be generous and willing to share. In this way, they will lay up treasure for themselves as a firm foundation for the coming age, so that they may take hold of the life that is truly life" (1 Tim. 6:18–19). God's promise is "A generous man will prosper; he who refreshes others will himself be refreshed" (Prov. 11:25). As opposed to the people of the world, the Christian should be known for his generosity and not his greed.

Worry (Matt. 6:25–34)

Worry! My, how the world worries. When there is doubt; when there is uncertainty; when it looks like you may not get the result you want: the world worries. What if...? What if...? According to our Lord, the Christian should not be like the world and this is one area where the difference should really be evident. The worldly person worries; the Christian is not to worry.

Jesus tells us two things about physical needs: the worldly people are preoccupied with them; and, our heavenly Father knows we need them. According to Phil. 4:19 God has promised to supply all our needs. If we don't believe that and act accordingly (by not worrying) we are "of little faith." In other words, worrying shows a lack of faith in God. For the Christian, that is sin (Rom. 14:23).

All of this is not to say that the Christian should not work for their food. The Bible says we should (2 Thess. 3:10). God does not actually feed the birds. He makes food available but they have to feed themselves. God uses "means" to meet the needs of birds (seeds, bugs, etc) and flowers (sun, minerals in soil, etc.) and He will use "means" to meet our needs. What those means are we may not know until the last minute; but the means will arrive and God should be given the glory.

Also, all of this is not to say that freedom from worry means freedom from trouble and tribulation. Jesus said: "Each day has enough trouble of its own." In John 16:33 Jesus said: "I have told you these things, so that in me you may have peace. In this world you will have trouble. But take heart! I have overcome the world." You cannot have peace and take heart if you are full of worry about the things of this life. Jesus has overcome the troubles of this world and we are "in Christ" (1 Cor. 1:30). When trouble comes God will provide the means for us to get through it.

The main concern of our Lord in this teaching, and the thing that should be the Christian's main concern in the world, is our testimony. Does our life reflect our faith in the God that created all things, and sustains all things, and controls all things? When the worldly people see Christians worrying about things just like they do they realize that the Christian is no better off with God than they are without God. The Christian who gives that kind of testimony is a false Christian because it is a false testimony. The Christian's light will shine brightest in the world when the storms come and he has peace because he is not worried about it.

Storms (Matt. 7:24–27)

Throughout the Sermon on the Mount Jesus is contrasting the true Christian to the merely religious person who is not really born again. In this section Jesus is talking about those who profess to be His followers. They sit under His teaching, whether on the mountainside in His day or in churches today. Some are true born-again Christians. Others are religious but not regenerated—they are false Christians. They may think they are true Christians, but they are deceived.

According to Jesus, the difference between the true Christian and the false Christian lies not in the hearing of His words, but in the doing of them. The difference in the two becomes evident when storms come into their lives. Most commentators view this parable as speaking of the final judgment of one's life. If it was built on the foundation of Jesus Christ, it indicates a true Christian, one that will stand up under the final judgment. If that life was not built on the foundation of Jesus Christ, it indicates a false Christian and that life will be condemned to destruction at the final judgment.

In this chapter on the Christian living in the world and being watched by the world we are going to interpret the parable in terms of the various storms that come into our lives as we are living in this world. As was said in the previous section, we all have troubles in this world. Some are small and come as light rain, but some are huge and come as Category 5 storms. The world watches the Christian to see how he handles the storms of life. Again, our testimony and God's image in the world is at stake.

There should be a big difference in the way a Christian handles the storms of life and how the non-Christian handles them. When a big storm comes to the life of a non-Christian their first reaction is usually selfish. "Woe is me!" "Why me?" "What did I do to deserve this?" "Life is not fair!" Those are legitimate reactions if a person does not believe in God and is not a child of God through faith in Jesus Christ. That person is of the world and has the expectation that the world will treat them fairly. They have no notion of what sin has done to the world and that the world they call home is under the control of Satan, the evil one, who comes to steal, kill, and destroy. So when their lives are destroyed by a storm they are only being treated as a member of the fallen world's family.

How different should be the way storms affect the lives of the family of God. The two lives may look the same on the outside. It consists of family, work, school, leisure, etc. The difference is how the life is lived, which is determined by the foundation upon which the life is built. When storms come nothing is as important as the foundation.

The life built on the world's sand is wonderful as long as the sun shines, but it collapses when the storm comes. If the Christian collapses in the storm where is the difference? The Christian is not to fear or worry when in the storms of life because he has a life built on a trust in God and His word. The word of God contains many, many promises that God will be with you in the storm and will help see you through the storm. "God is our refuge and strength, an ever-present help in trouble" (Ps. 46:1).

These promises are scattered throughout God's word just as the trees in a forest are hiding bird's nests among the leaves. You don't notice them unless you are looking for them. When a storm comes every bird knows where its own appropriate nest is and they fly to it. So God's promises in the Bible are hidden among the verses. We should fly to them, believe them, and hold fast to them until they are kept and the storm passes.

God has something else to say to us regarding His promises to help us when the storms come. We are to "...imitate those who through faith and patience inherit what has been promised" (Heb. 6:12). God makes a promise. Faith believes the promise. Hope anticipates the promise. Patience awaits the promise. At the appointed time we inherit the promise—it is a reality in our lives. When you pass through the storm let the world see you hold your head up high and not be afraid of the outcome because there is this promise: "And we know that in all things God works for the good of those who love him, who have been called according to his purpose" (Rom. 8:28).

The World is Watching

This chapter has been about the Christian living in the world. Christianity is an individual faith and the world pays close attention to those who claim to be Christian. The Christian is the only Christ they will see in this world. The world looks at Christians and gets its impression of Christianity, Christ and God. The world is looking for signs of hypocrisy. Therefore, how a Christian lives in the world is of utmost importance.

As seen earlier in this chapter, the world is watching to see how the Christian deals with anger and disagreements, honesty and generosity, relationships, pride, worry and storms. The Christian will encounter the same types of situations that the non-Christian encounters. The Christian will lose his job; the doctor's report will be bad; the loved one will die; the child will become an addict; the storms will come. The Christian will be hurt and the world will be watching. We, as children of God, must remember that hurt is not harm. Hurt is temporary. Harm is permanent. We have no promises from God that we will not be hurt. We do have promises that we will not be harmed. "If you make the Most High your dwelling–even the Lord, who is my refuge–10 then no harm will befall you, no disaster will come near your tent" (Ps. 91:9–10). Therefore, do not worry as the worldly people do.

Throughout the Sermon on the Mount the Lord has called His people to be different from everybody else in the world. We are different and we are to act different. The Christian is to live right in a world gone wrong in a way that is completely different from the way of the world. Jesus Christ has called us to renounce the ways of the prevailing secular culture and live the Christian counter-culture. Then when the world watches a Christian it will see Christ.

CHAPTER 8

Living Right in a World of Woe

"Whatever happens, conduct yourselves in a manner worthy of the gospel of Christ."(Phil. 1:27)

What does it mean to "conduct yourselves in a manner worthy of the gospel of Christ"? Christians live in a world that, in its heart, hates Christ, and therefore, hates Christians (John 15:18–19). It is a world gone wrong and a world of woe. The world watches the Christian as the Pharisees watched Christ looking for any hint of sin or hypocrisy. If the world sees sin in the life of a Christian it immediately discounts the gospel of Christ. That is because the world does not understand and believe the forgiveness aspect of the gospel of Christ. It only understands the strict morality of Christianity.

Conducting ourselves in a manner worthy of the gospel of Christ does entail living by a different moral standard than the world uses on itself. This chapter will present an overview of what the Bible says about the Christian living in the world and will conclude with some practical, and hopefully, helpful guidance for living as a Christian in the home and in society. The Greek word (*politeuomai*) is translated "conduct yourselves" in the above verse. In normal usage it is a political term used to refer to a citizen of a political state behaving like a citizen of that particular state ought to in order to not bring a reproach to that state. What comes to mind is citizens of America and the reputation they have overseas—"Those crazy Americans!" Of course, the usage here in the New Testament is referring to citizens of the Kingdom of God as they live in the world. The concept in its political and biblical usage includes fulfilling one's duty to the country or kingdom that one is a citizen of. In the Kingdom of God our conduct is to be shaped by what we believe about the gospel of Christ and the Christ of the gospel who saved us. We are not to bring a reproach to His name.

"Whoever claims to live in him must walk as Jesus did" (1 John 2:6). Another word the New Testament uses frequently to refer to our conduct is the word "walk". It is the translation of a Greek word (*peripateō*) that means to walk around, to live out, or to conduct one's life. In the New Testament it means the walk of life, the way that we live life. To walk means to live. Before the world, Christians are to:

Walk in newness of life (Rom. 6:4)
Walk by faith (2 Cor. 5:7)
Walk by the Spirit (Gal. 5:16)
Walk in the light (1 John 1:7)
Walk in obedience to His commands (2 John 6)

Walk in love (2 John 6)
Walk in the truth (3 John 3)
Live lives worthy of the calling we have received (Eph. 4:1)
Live as children of light (Eph. 5:8)
Live lives worthy of the Lord (Col. 1:10)
Live lives worthy of God (1 Thess. 2:12)

This is the way Jesus lived in the world in the first century and this is the way Christians are to live in the world in the twenty-first century. So how do we do it?

As stated earlier, the world only understands the strict morality associated with being a Christian. There is a morality involved and it does have a higher standard than the world. However, for the Christian, God's commands regarding morality are not burdensome (1 John 5:3). They are in keeping with the new life we have in Christ, and Christ in us means the commands are not only not burdensome, but they are possible to keep and a pleasure to obey. Before we get to the particulars of walking or living as a Christian in this world, we will look closer at what morality is and more importantly, at what the source of morals is for the Christian as opposed to the world.

The questions about morals and morality that Christians are confronted with most often in the world is "Who makes the rules?" and "What standard do you use?" For many non-Christians the law of the land determines: if it is not illegal, it is not immoral. The U.S. Supreme Court can determine what is legal, but it cannot determine what is moral. For others it is society at large. If most people approve it, it must be moral. For most non-Christians today morality is self-determining: "If I want to do it, it is the right thing for me." Of course, this kind of morality is the source of many problems in interpersonal relationships in the world. Morality is not the same from society to society or even from person to person in the same society. Adultery may no longer be against the law of the land but if one man takes another man's wife there are problems. If an adult determines it is right for him to have sex with a child there are problems. If man lives by man-made rules of behavior there are problems because man is fallen and is basically sinful.

What the world needs is a set of rules for behavior that are good for society and that do not cause problems in interpersonal relationships. These rules would have to be based upon something other than man, as man is sinful and self-centered. The world has such a set of rules and the standard used to set the rules is perfect and the basis of the standard is love. The rules are in the Bible and the standard for the rules is the character of the God of the Bible. The Bible sets forth right and wrong behavior for the Christian in the world.

We have previously in this work looked at the kind of person God wants a Christian to be in the world and some guidelines from the Sermon on the Mount for Christians living in the world. The rest of this chapter will offer some practical helps for being a good Christian in this world of woe and for resisting the temptations to sin that this world offers.

Being a Good Christian in the Home and in Society

> "Unless the Lord builds the house,
> its builders labor in vain" (Ps. 127:1a).

This verse does not refer to the Lord physically building a house but to a house (family) built upon the

Lord's principles for each member of the family as found in the Bible. Christian character begins in the home where people are intimately known. A Christian home is defined by what the parents are and do, and the Bible gives instructions for husbands, wives and children as they live as a Christian family in the home and as Christians in society. The most complete description of the roles of family members is found in Ephesians 5:15 to 6:4. I have purposely included verses 15–21 even though they are not normally included when quoted regarding the roles of husbands, wives and children. However, they offer some very practical instructions for being the kind of person that is a good Christian in society and a good husband or wife in a Christian family.

> Be very careful, then, how you live-not as unwise but as wise, 16 making the most of every opportunity, because the days are evil. 17 Therefore do not be foolish, but understand what the Lord's will is. 18 Do not get drunk on wine, which leads to debauchery. Instead, be filled with the Spirit. 19 Speak to one another with psalms, hymns and spiritual songs. Sing and make music in your heart to the Lord, 20 always giving thanks to God the Father for everything, in the name of our Lord Jesus Christ.
>
> 21 Submit to one another out of reverence for Christ.
>
> 22 Wives, submit to your husbands as to the Lord. 23 For the husband is the head of the wife as Christ is the head of the church, his body, of which he is the Savior. 24 Now as the church submits to Christ, so also wives should submit to their husbands in everything.
>
> 25 Husbands, love your wives, just as Christ loved the church and gave himself up for her 26 to make her holy,

cleansing her by the washing with water through the word, 27 and to present her to himself as a radiant church, without stain or wrinkle or any other blemish, but holy and blameless. 28 In this same way, husbands ought to love their wives as their own bodies. He who loves his wife loves himself. 29 After all, no one ever hated his own body, but he feeds and cares for it, just as Christ does the church- 30 for we are members of his body. 31 "For this reason a man will leave his father and mother and be united to his wife and the two will become one flesh." 32 This is a profound mystery-but I am talking about Christ and the church. 33 However, each one of you also must love his wife as he loves himself, and the wife must respect her husband.

6:1 Children, obey your parents in the Lord, for this is right. 2 "Honor your father and mother"-which is the first commandment with a promise- 3 "that it may go well with you and that you may enjoy long life on the earth."

4 Fathers, do not exasperate your children; instead, bring them up in the training and instruction of the Lord (Eph 5:15–6:4).

    First, verses 15–21 give some general guidelines required of good Christians in the home and in the world. The first directive is to be careful how you live. Don't just let life flow on without giving thought to how you are living it. Remember, "bad company corrupts good character" (1 Cor. 15:33). The next directive is to know the Lord's will with the implication of doing it after you know it. Prayer and Bible study are necessary in knowing the Lord's will. Chapter 3 contains some helpful guidelines in knowing God's will.

Next follows a warning about drunkenness. To be drunk affects among other things, how you walk and talk. The directive is to walk in the Spirit, that is, led by the Holy Spirit and giving thanks to God. Whatever comes our way, our response should be to give thanks to God with our talk. That testifies to all who hear us that we know God is directing our lives.

Living in society and in the home, Christians should be considerate, sympathetic, compassionate and humble as we live in harmony with everyone. In Titus 2 there is the command to be self-controlled. That goes back to being careful how you live. From Colossians 3, Christians are to clothe themselves with kindness, gentleness and patience, doing everything in the name of the Lord. That is, once the world knows you are a Christian, everything you do will be judged as reflecting Christ. Christians are to put on love (see Chapter 7).

If every Christian husband, wife and child was this kind of person and lived this way, homes would be heaven, society would be peaceful, and Christ would be glorified in the world. Now we will look at some specific instructions for husbands, wives and children from the above scriptures. The model for the husband-wife relationship is the relationship between Christ and His church.

Being a good Christian in the home

The following verses have also been consulted for attributes that husbands and wives ought to exhibit in the home as good Christians: Prov. 12:4; Eph. 4:26–27; Col. 3:12–21; 1 Pet. 3:1–9; 1 Tim. 3:1–13; 1 Tim. 5:7–8; Titus 2:1–6. In presenting the biblical mandates, the commandments will be divided between general responsibilities and specific commandments for husbands, wives and children.

The home is the place where the ideal Christian character should be exhibited as one lives before the Lord and before the one we loved enough to marry.

HUSBANDS – Husbands are head of the wife and family just as Christ is the head of the church. Headship means leadership. Headship means authority. Headship means responsibility. Headship means sacrifice. The role model for the husband in his role of headship is Christ. The husband's leadership should reflect Christ's leadership of the church. Christ has supreme authority over the church just as the husband has authority over the wife and children. Any diminishing of the husband's authority by the wife is a diminishing of the authority of Christ over His church.

With the husband's authority comes responsibility. The husband is responsible for the well-being of the wife (and children) just as he is responsible for the well-being of his own body. Well-being includes all aspects of being; spiritual, emotional and physical. Responsibility includes accountability for his behavior, his time, his stewardship of money and other assets.

The husband needs to be aware of his own behavior. His wife and children are watching him. He is setting the example for the family. If the husband is free with money, the wife will tend to be free with money. If the husband is irritable, the wife will tend to be irritable. If the husband smokes, the son will tend to smoke when grown. If the husband abuses alcohol, the son will tend to abuse alcohol when grown. If the husband abuses the wife, the son will tend to abuse his wife when grown. And if the husband does Bible studies and prays with the family, the son will tend to have Bible studies and pray with his family when grown. If the husband tenderly loves and cares for his wife, the son will tend to tenderly love and care for his wife when grown. The husband's behavior toward the wife also influences the daughter's relationship with their husband when they are grown. The example of the husband is extremely important and sets the model for behavior of the family members just as Christ is the model for the Church.

The husband needs to be a hands-on manager of the family. He should be aware of what is going on in the lives of his wife and children by having frequent and open communication. Just as Jesus could always pray to the Father, the wife and children should have open access to the husband and father. He should keep his household under control (1 Tim. 3:4–5) making sure what needs to happen happens, and what does not need to happen does not happen.

The husband is responsible for setting a loving atmosphere and a Christian environment in the home, and in consultation with the wife, setting the rules of the home. He needs to monitor the gates to the home (guests, television, music, radio, Internet) to make sure no ungodly things enter in. Romans 14:22b applies here: "Blessed is the man who does not condemn himself by what he approves." The husband has the authority to keep the home godly and if he allows ungodly things to enter he is in essence approving them.

With responsibility comes the responsibility to provide for the wife and children (1 Tim. 5:8). The husband is to provide for physical needs of food, clothing and shelter. He is also to provide the spiritual needs by taking the leadership in Bible study, prayer, worship and church attendance. He is to meet the emotional needs by loving as Christ loved the church and gave himself for her. The needs of the wife become the needs of the husband. The needs of the children become the needs of the husband/father. If it is important for any member of the family, it is important to the husband. In this age where wants have become needs, with so many wives needing to work outside the home to help supply the needs of the family, the husband has more pressure to meet the spiritual and emotional needs of the family. His own work means spending a majority of his time away from the family and home. When the wife works she has less time for the family and home. Allowing the wife to work does not relieve the husband of any of his responsibility of headship and it makes it much harder for him to meet his God-given responsibilities.

The husband is to love his wife as if she were his own body, as if she were he: "he who loves his wife loves himself." The husband feeds and cares for his own body. If he has pain he does something about it. When his flesh "cries out" he answers. In the same way he must answer when his wife "cries out" giving her priority over himself. He should also give her priority over his own father and mother. The wife is to be just as important to the husband as the husband is to himself because the two have become one flesh. The wife is to be treated with consideration and respect by the husband as they both share the same flesh and are joint-heirs in the same eternal life.

If there are children in the family the husband must not exasperate his children (Eph. 6:4). To exasperate means to excite the anger of; to cause irritation or annoyance, usually when the children feel like they can do nothing to help the situation. Instead of exasperating the children, the husband should bring them up in the training and instruction of the Lord. That includes training them how to handle exasperation by taking it to the Lord in prayer and by forgiving and enduring. The Lord's way is the way of love. Likewise, the father is not to embitter his children, "or they will become discouraged" (Col. 3:21). This is basically saying that father should not make their children bitter, that is, grievous, distressful, causing pain to the point that the child is characterized by intense antagonism or hostility. Nothing discourages a child like feelings of hostility toward a parent. They know that is not the way to feel toward a parent and they feel guilty for feeling that way. The father's responsibility is to instruct the child and discipline the child in a tender loving way so that the end result is a feeling of security for the child, not a feeling of hostility.

The responsibility of headship on the husband is the same as on Christ as head of the church. It cost Christ His life. It will also cost the husband his.

WIVES – The Bible has much less to say about the role of the wife than about the role of the husband. In Ephesians 5 we are told that the marriage relationship is built on the pattern of the relationship between Christ and His Church with the role of Christ being the example for the role of the husband and the role of the Church being the example of the role of the wife. As we have seen, the role of the husband, as it is with the role of Christ, is the role of headship, authority, responsibility, and sacrifice. The burden of the relationship rests on Christ and on the husband. The role of the wife, as is the role of the church, is to submit to the headship provided: husband for the wife, Christ for the Church.

> Wives, submit to your husband as to the Lord. 23 For the husband is the head of the wife as Christ is the head of the church, his body, of which he is Savior. 24 Now as the church

submits to Christ, so also wives should submit to their husband in everything (Eph. 5:22–24).

The church has no problem submitting to Christ because of all He has done for the Church, dying for it, sending His Spirit to guide it. What would not a person do for someone who saved his life? Christ saved us from Hell and the eternal life we have is all due to Him—so we submit willingly and joyfully to Him. If the husband is doing for the wife all that his role of headship requires, the wife should have no problem submitting to him willingly and joyfully.

The wife is also given the command to respect her husband. She is not only to respect his role as head of her and the family; she should respect him as a person. The husband, of course, should be worthy of respect, and he will be, if he faithfully performs his role as husband and loves his wife as Christ loved the Church and gave Himself up for her.

Scripture gives some guidelines for the wife for the kind of person she should be and the kind of duties and responsibilities she has as wife and mother. Proverbs 31 gives a good biblical description of a "wife of noble character." In reading down the description we find that the husband has full confidence in her; she brings him good, not harm; she brings respect to her husband; she is dignified; she is wise; she watches over the affairs of her household. She performs her role to such an extent that her children bless her and her husband praises her. "A wife of noble character is her husband's crown, but a disgraceful wife is like decay to his bones" (Prov. 12:4).

Proverbs 31 also says the noble wife is clothed with strength. That is a reminder that submission is not a sign of weakness. It is wisdom to obey the Lord and it is beauty to God's eyes and brings the wife great worth.

Instead, it [beauty] should be that of your inner self, the unfading beauty of a gentle and quiet spirit, which is of great worth in God's sight. 5 For this is the way the holy women of the past who put their hope in God used to make themselves beautiful. They were submissive to their own husbands (1 Peter 3:4–5).

The wife who fulfils her role by submitting and respecting her husband and by having a noble character is a treasure to her husband. "A wife of noble character who can find? She is worth far more than rubies" (Prov. 31:10).

CHILDREN – The biblical role for children is very simple and is stated twice in the New Testament.

> Children, obey your parents in everything, for this pleases the Lord (Col. 3:20).
>
> Children, obey your parents in the Lord, for this is right. 2 "Honor your father and mother" – which is the first commandment with a promise – 3 "that it may go well with you and that you may enjoy long life on the earth" (Eph. 6:1–3).

Children have to be taught to obey the father and mother. It is the responsibility of the father and mother to teach them to obey. This pleases the Lord and keeps the children from sinning in this area. As the children grow they become responsible for their own obedience to their parents. If they are brought up with the training and instruction of the Lord, obeying their parents is what they will want to do.

Here in the twenty-first century many children are growing to adulthood but are not leaving their parents household. If the child is an adult living with his or her parents, does the commandment stand? Does their relationship change? The way parents communicate to grown sons and daughters will change from the way they communicated to them as children. What does not change is the father's headship and responsibility to maintain a godly Christian environment in the home. He is still responsible to guard the gates to the home.

Another thing that does not change is the obligation of grown sons and daughters to honor their fathers and mothers. The promise that comes with this commandment is conditional and lasts as long as the father or mother is still alive. The promise is "that it may go well with you and that you may enjoy long life on the earth." The grown son or daughter living with their parents is obligated to honor the headship and authority of the father as long as they are in the father's house. If only the mother is living she inherits the headship and all that applied to the husband/father now applies to her. However, she is now due more respect and care because she is a widow.

Being a good Christian in society

Remember it was said earlier that the world is watching the Christian. The Christian in society is under closer scrutiny than criminals or lunatics. The world is looking for hypocrisy, bigotry and signs that we are like them so they can say, "Why be a Christian?" It is important to remember that we do image the unchangeable God in a world that is constantly changing for the worse.

The Church and the Christian home are the only two places in society that should be accepting, safe and unchanging. Deep down every person wants acceptance, security and stability. Christians are the only ones that have that in society. Christians are the only people in society that God expects to seek first His kingdom and His righteousness. A good Christian will do that and will be noticeably different from others in society.

To be different, the Christian's attitude toward material things should be different from the world's. The world says, "It's mine" and the more you get the happier you will be. The reality of it is just the opposite. The more you get the more you want. According to James 4:1–2 this desire for things we do not have causes quarrels and fights among people of the world. The Christian's attitude toward material things should be that given in 1 Cor. 7:30–31: "...those who buy something, [should live] as if it was not theirs to keep; those who use the things of the world, as if not engrossed in them. For this world in its present form is passing away." Hold things loosely in your hands and you will be different from society.

This naturally leads into the Christian's attitude toward money and how it should be different from those in the society around you. The world loves money. Hebrews 13:5 tells Christians, "Keep your lives free from the love of money and be content with what you have, because God has said, 'Never will I leave you; never will I forsake you.'" Christians have a God who has promised to supply all of our needs. We do not need money for ourselves alone, we need it to use for others for God's glory. That is the way to use money to store up treasures in Heaven. That same scripture in Matthew 6 says that we cannot serve two masters; we cannot serve both God and money. Money can master you by capturing your heart and by capturing your mind making you worry about it. Society is full of people worrying about money and the things they want but cannot buy. Statistics show that more married couples in our society argue over money than any other thing. Christians are not to be like other people in our society in our attitude toward money.

Another area of society in which there should be a marked difference in Christians is in our attitude toward and involvement in sexual relations. There is now a major boundary line in sexual relations. Christians are on one side of the line and society is on the other. That boundary line separates natural and unnatural sexual activity. On the natural side of the sexual relations boundary, there are moral boundaries governing who it is proper to have sexual relations with. It is considered to be immoral to have sexual relations with anyone who is not your spouse, with children, family members, animals, etc. On the unnatural side of the boundary line, there are no other boundaries. Homosexuality, pedophilia, bestiality are all together on the unnatural side of the boundary. On that side of the boundary line if one is good why would not another be good? There is nothing to differentiate between sexual relations except personal preference.

God has put boundaries around the Christian's sexual relations and they represent the opposite of society's view. Society no longer has any boundaries. It used to be in society that dating was for the purpose of looking for a prospective spouse. In society today dating is for the purpose of having sexual relations. For Christians, sexual relations are for expressing intimacy between a man and woman who are married. How far removed has society become from God's standard! The good Christian should not conform to the world in the area of sexual relations. A Christian should avoid circumstances that would tempt toward immorality or that would give the appearance of ungodly relations with the opposite sex. Early in his ministry, Billy Graham adopted a rule that served him well in public life. He would never be alone with a member of the opposite sex in a restaurant, a car, an elevator or a room. In such situations, the world will assume there is more to the relationship than business or ministry.

The Christian in society must not conform to society. Many church leaders are bowing to conformity with society in the area of sexual relations especially after the U.S. Supreme Court decision not only legalizing, but ordering, same-sex marriages in all states. The Christian in society must be governed by Romans 12:2: "Do not conform any longer to the pattern of this world, but be transformed by the renewing of your mind. Then you will be able to test and approve what God's will is—His good, pleasing and perfect will." "The world and its desires pass away, but the man who does the will of God lives forever." 1 John 2:17.

Conclusion

Living right is all about being a good Christian in this world of woe. We have seen that it is a world of woe because it is wrong. It calls evil good and good evil. It puts darkness for light, and light for darkness. We have seen how it went wrong and what is wrong with it today. In this chapter we have looked at being a good Christian in this world of woe, both at home and in society. Remember, Jesus is our example of being a good Christian in the world and "whoever claims to be in him must walk as Jesus did"

(1 John 2:6). In the Bible, the word "walk" is used to mean how one lives their life; their character and their conduct.

Jesus walked in righteous opposition to the prevailing culture of His day. He was persecuted and crucified for it. The Christian today must also walk in righteous opposition to the prevailing ungodly culture. The world gone wrong will not lie down in the face of righteous opposition. It will fight back with all the weapons at its disposal. These weapons include verbal abuse, persecution and imprisonment and even death to those who oppose it. Christian, are you prepared to pay that price? You will be if Jesus Christ is your life. His life, your life. His death, your death. His resurrection to eternal life, your resurrection to eternal life. Be of good cheer, Christian, for you have overcome this world of woe.

Ivory Palaces

1. My Lord has garments so wondrous fine,
   And myrrh their texture fills;
   Its fragrance reached to this heart of mine
   With joy my being thrills.
   - Refrain:
     Out of the ivory palaces,
     Into **a world of woe**,
     Only His great eternal love
     Made my Savior go.
2. His life had also its sorrows sore,
   For aloes had a part;
   And when I think of the cross He bore,
   My eyes with teardrops start.
3. His garments, too, were in cassia dipped,
   With healing in a touch;
   In paths of sin had my feet e'er slipped—
   He's saved me from its clutch.
4. In garments glorious He will come,
   To open wide the door;
   And I shall enter my heav'nly home,
   To dwell forevermore.

Henry Barraclough
Public Domain

www.ingramcontent.com/pod-product-compliance
Lightning Source LLC
Chambersburg PA
CBHW070629300426
44113CB00010B/1712